C000145255

The Second Wave

My Surfing Life - The Saltburn Way

Jon Metcalfe

Spire Publishing - December 2010

Copyright © Jon Metcalfe

This book is sold subject to the condition that it shall not, by way of trade or otherwise, be lent, resold, hired out, or otherwise circulated without the publisher's prior consent in any form of binding or cover other than that in which it was published and without a similar condition including this condition being imposed on the subsequent publisher.

The moral right of Jon Metcalfe
to be identified as the author of this work has been asserted.

First published in Canada and the UK 2010
by Spire Publishing Ltd.

A cataloguing record for this book is available from the Library and Archives Canada.
Visit www.collectionscanada.ca/amicus/index-e.html

Printed and bound in the USA or the UK
by Lightning Source Ltd.

ISBN: 978-1-926635-51-4

Spire Publishing
www.spirepublishing.com

FOR

GILL, JAMES AND LAURA

INDEX

MY SUB-TITLE

"YOU MUST BE BLOODY MAD!!!"

This is an often heard phrase used up and down the North East coast. Said by total strangers, as you struggle in / out of your wetsuit. Before / after a Winters surf session.

Jon Metcalfe

THE INTRO

The anticipation that you feel as you head off towards Saltburn, in the hope of surf, is for me a gut wrenching experience.

Desperately hoping a storm hundreds of miles away has generated a swell to bring waves.

As you get closer to the top of the bank, with a vehicle loaded down with boards and wetsuits, the butterflies really start to kick in.

The first sight of the point in the distance tells all.

Over the brow of the hill, the point is working, Penny's and the beach.

Lines of surf, a light offshore wind...the start of another Saltburn surfing weekend.

Welcome to my book.

As you will soon discover, this is not your typical surfing book.

It's about how I became a surfer and I'm proud to say a Longboarder.

Let me start by saying, I'm not a particularly good exponent of the surfing art but an enthusiastic one.

I am an average British surfer, a person who is not easily put off by the freezing North Sea and a fair share of sewage. Testing conditions to say the least.

It would be easy to surf in warmer climbs Hawaii, Fiji, Brazil, Cornwall but this is my home and I love it, no matter what.

9

I have been told, that to surf year round on the North East coast is "Character building", I prefer to think of it as a passionate madness, an obsession, an addiction.

In the book, I have tried to be down to earth and honest as much as possible.

It does contain some swear words and sexual references but don't let that put you off.

I have tried to keep it roughly in chronological order, with a couple of exceptions, when I go off at a tangent.

Just to warn you, some of the facts might be a bit dodgy in places, some stories have been altered or omitted to protect the innocent.

I have, however, tried to keep it "real", it is a bit fragmented, so be warned.

If I had left all the "juicy" bits in this book, it would have been three times as long and I would have been locked up.

So this is all your going to get.

If you don't like the words then just look at the pictures.

Hopefully, it will inspire you to get up off your arse and give surfing a go.

It's now very easy to buy or hire a wetsuit and board.

Don't stand back and say "the sea is too cold" or utter one of the million and one excuses that keeps you out of the water because one day you will look back and regret it.

TRY SURFING IT WILL CHANGE YOUR LIFE

For me the mid 1980's were key years in my life but I hadn't realised.

My generation should have been very depressed.

We had Thatcherism, riots in the streets, strikes close to home, huge unemployment and AIDS.

There was no future.

I had managed to secure a job after my apprenticeship, the wonderful world of British Steel awaited.

"It's a job for life", people told me.

I was surrounded by heavy industry, so the choice was either steel or chemicals? Easy as that.

We saved the world with Live Aid, watching it on one of only 4 T.V. channels.

Middlesbrough F.C. the team I had followed home and away for years, were now struggling.

Even in the third division, the basement of English football, the craic was brilliant.

If your a Boro fan you have to be an eternal optimist.

With Bruce Rioch as manager and financial vultures gathering, it was all doom and gloom.

The gates to Ayresome Park were locked, the fat lady was about to sing. I sent in £10 to save the club.

Computers and mobile phones were around but were big and expensive. Who needed them anyway.

A lot of things were changing...

Myself and my friends had no idea that we were entering a "Golden age" of surfing at Saltburn.

By that I mean, a lot of people started surfing within a couple of years of us. It was when the sport really took off in a big way.

We were the second wave of surfing enthusiasts at Saltburn, there were a few pioneers that paved the way for us.

They had started the ball rolling in the 1960's but for one reason or another surfing didn't explode until later.

We slowly built up a strong surfing community, everyone knew everyone.

Inside that community we formed a small group, a family a close band of like minded individuals with a love of life and addiction for waves.

In Saltburn, we had discovered a special place, an "island", where we had everything at our fingertips. Everything a young surfer could ever want, all within 200 yards.

There was a pub, a good nightclub, the carpark for living in cars and vans, a pier and Huncliff for eye pleasing beauty, the beach and plenty of waves.

At the time of writing this book that was around 25 years ago, when it all began. It seems like yesterday.

O.K. brace yourself, this is the boring bit about me.

I come from a village on the North East coast of England.
Marske-by-the-Sea.

Thanks to my Mam and Dad, I was born and have always lived within half a mile of the sea.

It's always been there, luring me since I was born.

My Dad took me fishing from an early age.

We would go sea-fishing with his friends on various boats like the Valkyrie, Argus and Coquet Queen.

Sometimes it was like a mill pond but on other occasions huge swells would come from the North bringing snow and hail. I loved every second of it.

It gave me a new prospective on the sea, its beauty and ferocity.

I was mesmerised.

We would trawl for bait for a couple of hours, check and re-bait lobster pots then we would fish for hours. Changing position to find where the fish were.

On the journey back to shore, the diesel engines throbbing tones and the fumes always knocked me out. I would awake as the tractor pulled us up the beach.

I started writing many years ago.

When I discovered surfing, I sent photos and bits of stories away.

Paul Knowles, from East Kent, started to print them in his quarterly publication "Surfs Up."

A true grass roots magazine.

THE SOUL OF SURFING   ISSUE 16 SUMMER 1994

He encouraged surfers to write about their experiences, trips and lifestyles.

It was a very readable magazine and much appreciated by the longboarders.

Unfortunately, due to unforeseen circumstances the magazine folded, (no pun intended), leaving only the glossies.

Surf magazine, Wavelength and later Carve did print a few bits and pieces about Saltburn, using some of my photos and short bits from the lads, but they concentrated on the chosen few surfing in exotic places. Places we could only dream of.

We still bought them, as any fix would do, but they gave only limited information about what was going on at grass roots level in the U.K.

I have read so many books about surfing, enjoying most, that I decided to give it a go myself.

This is it.

After many years and many re-writes, this is the result.

If you think its good, bad or indifferent, I don't really care.

If it helps one person stop watching T.V. or playing on their X box and get in the water then it would have been worth it.

If you want to read a more historically accurate book about Saltburn Surfers then read "Don't jump off the pier" by Simon Palmer.

It's a well written book on a subject close to my heart.

My surfing base is in Saltburn, a place sandwiched between "smoggy" industrial Teesside and the North Yorkshire countryside.

Saltburn is populated by an eclectic mix of people and characters.

As a very broad generalisation, there are the well off folk, the artistic folk, the people who think that they are well off, normal salt of the earth people, people struggling on the bread line and of course the scum of the earth.

All seem a bit eccentric, I suspect there's something in the water.

Everyone though, has a good sense of humour.

There are huge Victorian houses and the many bedsits in the Jewel streets, the whole world seems to be encapsulated here.

It is a wondrous area to grow up in, the "Smog" myth was only made up to keep people out and keep the waves uncrowded.

I hope you enjoy the rest of the book.

Welcome to "THE SECOND WAVE, MY SURFING LIFE, THE SALTBURN WAY"

THE BEGINNING

Surfing is about beautiful places, palm fringed white sand beaches, clear blue sea, perfectly formed waves. Hot lazy days...

KABOOM...

Back to reality, I'm hit by another wall of foaming white water.
I'm getting the whole of the cold North sea, flushed through my ill fitting, baggy wetsuit.
The arms and legs are now ballooned with the water. My balance is gone. I'm floundering about.
I start to question my sanity.
I slowly regain my composure, take a deep breath and try again, pushing myself further into the impact zone.

How the hell did I get into this...

It all started, when me and my best mate Tom, decided that we needed to do something different in our lives.
We were young, free and single and just wanted to have "fun."
I had known Tom and his brothers Ste and Peter from early days at infant school.
Their family moved around the corner from me and that was it best mates.

Time was spent with other friends, doing the usual kids stuff and getting into trouble.

We played football on "the Green" for hours at a time, winning World and F.A. cups, as we went.
Half time would be spent eating broken biscuits from Hills the bakers, washed down with Lowcocks lemonade.
Games ended in ridiculous score lines, 36 all wasn't uncommon.
It always ended with someone's Mam saying "tea was ready" or "it's dark, get yourself in."

One match was abandoned as Wool, one of the lads, broke his leg.
The ambulance drove onto the field and straight over our jumper goalposts.
Godba wasn't too happy, it was his new Brazil coloured tracksuit top.

15

The Green was also the venue for games of no holds barred Bulldog. Loads of kids would turn up and the game just kicked off.

Bloody noses, scratches and bruises were suffered by all.

Even the biggest, hardest kid was taken down and pounded, by a mass of ankle biters.

Bikes were ridden everywhere.

Suicidal jumps were made out of anything we could get our hands on but as we only had choppers or racing bikes, the accidents came thick and fast.

We spent a lot of time on the sand dunes and cliffs, building "dens" then attacking each other with rocks and stones.

Doing the same in the farmers field was more dangerous.

Dens were built out of square bails of hay. We attacked each other with straw root, mud bombs. Nothing unusual there.

If the farmer turned up, he wouldn't be in a playful mood. This usually ended up with everyone scattering, running for your lives pursued by a tractor or red faced farmer threatening to shoot us.

Around Bonfire night we would attack each other with fireworks.

Chucking bangers and aiming airbomb repeaters at each other.

We made "genies" from the gunpowder inside of a few fireworks.

They were lit at arms length and with a flash and a bang, everyone got temporary blindness for a few minutes.

The fireworks code was never followed.

Part of the local cliffs was used as a firing range, many years ago.

It was easy to find ammunition, of some description, littered about.

We did tried to set them off, hitting them with large stones, thankfully without success.

One large shell was taken to the local police station. One look and they nearly had kittens, the bomb squad arrived and took it away, they wouldn't tell us if they used stones to set it off.

Throwing arrows was another dangerous passing phase.

Hand crafted from garden sticks, sharpened for better aerodynamics and with playing cards as flights.

We launched them using thick string, knotted, securing it in a slot at the back of the arrow.

At first our best effort was 20 feet, rubbish.
We weighted the arrow, some using the end of a dart.
With practice, we now threw them over 150 feet.
It caused a fair bit of trouble when irate footballers got in our way...

Slightly safer we made dune boards, shaped pieces of plywood with a turned up nose.
We would attempt to ride these down the largest of sand dunes.
Running like hell and jumping onboard.
Everyone always ended up with mouthfuls of sand.

The Valley gardens, Saltburn and New Marske woods were also favourite places. There were always plenty of Tarzan ropes hanging and becks to jump or fall into.

We also did a lot of hanging around, being bored.
It was a normalish childhood.
Yes, we were idiots at times, but we got through it and just about survived.

As we grew older, most of us started watching bands. Touring the country to see the best.
We also went on scooter runs, all enjoying the all nighters and the craic. Sleeping rough was an acceptable hardship.

Skip a few years...

A few of us decided to have a lads weekend in the Lake district.
Hawkshead was our destination, as it sounded like a good place.
We weren't going for the National parks majestic beauty or for a visit to Coniston water, where Donald Campbell died, we were going for a piss up.
Myself, Tom, Ste, Dod, Tash, Greame and Dave, (friends from either school or the Frigate / Middle house pubs in Marske) set off.
Tom had managed to borrow his works van.
We cleaned it up a bit and loaded the essentials, lager, sleeping bags and porn magazines.
We made the trip over the A66 to Hawkshead.
The small Lakeland village made us very welcome.
We started at the Sun Inn pub and roamed to the Kings Arms, Queens Head and Red Lion and then back again.

We had a bit of banter with the locals as we went.

Passing a youth hostel, a couple of lasses shouted down from a top floor window, "Are any of you lot going to come up here?", blowing kisses.

We looked at each other and said something about them looking fit and asked how we could get in?

"Can't you get a ladder and climb up", came the reply.

Alarm bells started to ring, why didn't they just tell us where the front door was?

We shouted "How old are you?"

The reply came from a male voice, obviously in charge of them.

"They are nearly 15 and won't be having any visitors tonight, thank you."

Waving, we shouted back "see you in a few years", and then moved on to the next pub.

We had parked / abandoned the van by the banks of the lake. Wedged between two trees.

We all slept in the back of the van, conditions weren't ideal, a bit cramped.

Tempers soon frayed about snoring levels, I hadn't heard a thing.

Scuffles broke out.

A traffic cone, that had been acquired, was thrown around the back of the van.

Somewhat unjustly and with a few "fuck offs", myself and Tom were ejected from the van.

Outside wasn't as bad as we had expected. It was cold but with sleeping bags and 70 foot of plastic sheeting to keep us warm, it was a safer option than in the van.

At around 5 in the morning, we were woken by a knocking noise.

Tom then uttered the classic line "That's a male spotted woodpecker, you know!"

It was early morning, I'm wrapped in plastic, with a raging hangover, furry mouth, on the banks of a lake and Toms telling me about bloody lesser spotted woodpeckers.

Well I just pissed myself laughing.

The laughing didn't stop all weekend, drunken, piss taking all the way.

We toured around looking for a cafe which was open, we ended up in Ambleside.

It was still early morning and the place was like a ghost town, not even the newsagent was open.

The only thing that was open, was the pitch and putt.

Seven hungover, hungry people attempted to play golf could have gone down as a comedy classic, had anyone had the energy to film it.

The rain started to come down, we played on.

It got heavier, we play on until like drowned rats, we finished the last hole.

Very damp around the edges, we found a cafe.

We stuffed our faces and drank lots of coffee, the rain got heavier.

What are we going to do now? Was the question.

Everyone sat there blank.

An information board gave us the answer, Motor boats with cabins for hire.

We hired 2 small motor boats until pub opening time.

It seemed like a good way to kill a couple of hours.

Max speed turned out to be 4 MPH. We putt-putted around the lake.

After 10 minutes, we started to get bored.

Dod said he could "get it to go a lot faster" adding " he had worked on similar engines before."

Like fools we believed him.

In no time at all, we were floating powerless, in the middle of the lake. The engine partially stripped with the few tools in the boat.

The other boat had motored miles away in the distance.

We started to plead with Dod "just put it back together and we can get to the pub."

The reply was typical Dod "you can't hurry perfection."

We all looked at each other, all getting a bit pissed off with the situation.

Five minutes later and just as we were about to keelhaul Dod, he announced that it was back together.

He fired the engine up and accelerated to full speed.

"There you go" said Dod, puffing his chest out.

"What do you mean, that's fucking slower than before."

"Do you want me to have another go at it?"

No one replied but the looks could have killed.

We made it, eventually, to now dryish land.

The rest of the weekend went by in a bit of a blur.

It was spent drinking, swimming in freezing Coniston, (it seemed like a good idea at the time), drinking, playing football and more drinking.

We had a laugh with everyone we met, locals, tourists, walkers and of course all the barmaids.

On the journey back, someone mentioned that a van was hiring surfboards and wetsuits in Saltburn, about 2 miles from where we lived.

Now if we had gone straight to the Frigate, a favoured pub in Marske, this book would have never been written. We luckily went that extra mile (or two), and discovered something that would change our lives.

As we drove down Saltburn bank, we could see a large van with its back door rolled up.

Boards rested on the black railing. They pointed out to the 4 foot mushy waves in a grey / brown sewage sea.

As we parked up and got out, the roar of the sea grew louder.
It was cold and the smell of salt and shite hung in the air.
It was cold, bloody freezing, in fact.
These were not ideal conditions to start our surfing lives.

We hired boards and wetsuits and then the fun really started.
Looking back, we had all seen a bit of surfing on television, it all looked easy.
We were to find out that it wasn't.
You couldn't help but laugh as we struggled into our ill fitting wetsuits.
Some lay on their backs on the floor wriggling into them, while others whirled their arms like mad windmills.
One of the lads struggled for ages, eventually announcing that "its on" arms raised to show everyone.
What he hadn't realised that the zip was supposed to be at the back, not the front!

We all sucked our bellies in, as zips were secured.
My suit wasn't ideal, it was baggy under the arms and around the legs, surely that didn't really matter.
As we grabbed the boards the smell of coconut and strawberry filled our nostrils, the boards had been pre-waxed for us.
We velcroed our leashes around our ankles and headed into the sea.
Lambs to the slaughter.

Everyone did the little feet into cold sea dance, hopping from foot to foot.
The initial shock soon faded and then the battle against the white water started.
We stepped, jumped and pushed our boards further out.
Wave after wave pushed us back.
As I waded deeper, I got a flush of seawater down my back.
After a bit of shouting I continued further out.
No-one had thought about getting onto the board and paddling, at this very early stage in our surfing career.

A sideways glance at the pier told me that I hadn't got any further out in an hour.
I felt battered and a bit deflated, as others were a lot further out but I was determined to get beyond the breaking waves.

I thought I'd made it out back once. Wrong.

A big set came in and exploded, turning me and pushing me towards the beach at great speed.

I was a tiny piece of flotsam floating in a huge sea.

I held my board tightly as I rode the wave all the way, not even attempting to get to my feet.

I steered my board by shifting my body weight from side to side, sort of controlling my ride.

It felt brilliant being pushed beachward by the power of the wave.

Again and again, I repeated the process.

After 2 hours, our faces, feet and hands were bright red with the cold.

Fingers stiffened up, we all shook uncontrollably, hypothermia was setting in.

Most had tried and failed to get to their feet.

Our wipeouts, were slow-motion slapstick.

Time after time, we all rode the white water into the beach on our bellies.

We all managed to avoid the pier.

That was difficult as the current seemed to be sucking you into the metal pier legs.

We all made it through our first session. Tom was the only one to make it to his feet and actually ride a wave. An obvious natural, clever bastard.

I don't know if it was the cold or the surf or that we were completely burnt out after the weekend but all of us came out with the biggest grins that you have ever seen.

The feeling of elation wasn't just the weekend worth of drink this was something else.

Slightly predictably, we got changed and went to the nearest pub. Our van abandoned in the carpark.

Rosie O' Gradys had recently opened. A fine pub situated on a bank overlooking the beach and sea, ideal for wave watching.

It was a stylish place with shining brass fittings and art deco lamps. Loads of eye catching stuff on the walls and Billie Holiday playing non-stop through the sound system.

It was to become a home from home.

The time in the pub wasn't just spent talking about our Lakes trip.

It was spent going through our new found surfing adventure.

Wave by wave, beer by beer.

It was also spent admiring the barmaids.

This was the beginning of a life changing time, a time when we would make friendships that would last a lifetime.

Next day, at the Coil plate mill, Lackenby, where I worked, the usual questions were asked in our "tiffy" workshop.
Did you watch the Boro on Saturday?
What did you get up to this weekend?

I mentioned that I'd been over to the Lakes with the lads.
No reaction.
I then mentioned that I'd been surfing at Saltburn.
After a short pause and a few blank looks, the piss taking started.
I had lit the blue touch paper and was witnessing human fireworks.
"There's no surf at Saltburn, you daft git",
"Are you going to grow your hair, dye it blonde and listen to the Beach boys records",
"So your going to be a surfer dude" said in a sort of Scooby Doo Shaggy voice.
"Do you take your ironing board with you and do this."
Picture a middle aged bloke, standing on a table waving his arms in the air.

I hadn't expected any reaction at all. It was unusual to say the least.

THE FIRST STEPS

Over the next couple of months, all of our spare time was spent either in the sea, around the carpark or in Saltburns many pubs.

We introduced a few of our friends to the wonders of surfing.

Kev and Jeff, were amongst them.

Kev was enthusiastic, as he is about everything that he gets involved in.

He's an outdoor adventure type of lad, up for anything and game for a laugh.

Just as an example, he was sacked once for chasing a secretary around a workshop.

Nothing wrong with that.

Kev being Kev, was inside a 10 foot cardboard tube, only his arms and legs sticking out and a small slot to see through.

He was running around knocking stuff everywhere, chasing the lass.

What he didn't know was that his boss was watching from the balcony above.

Taxi for Kev.

Jeff, as normal, went at surfing gung-ho loving every minute in the water.

When we started surfing Jeff was in the Navy, so he had opportunity to surf in many exotic locations, where the rest of us could only dream of.

In Kenya, he found a reef break ½ mile offshore with some cracking waves.

After a short session, he started to loose feeling in his left hand.

After a short while, his left arm started to go numb.

He made the long paddle in, by the time he got to the beach he was paralysed down the left side of his body.

A visit to a local doctor soon sorted the problem out. He'd been stung by a poisonous fish and hadn't realised.

He didn't hurry back in the water.

Slowly we got to know the "proper" surfers and other grommets, like us.

Nick and Gary from the van / shop, Vince, Nick and Lisa Markl, Al Smith, Chris Harbisher, Scottish Robbie and many others.

They always made us feel very welcome, giving us tips from wetsuits to styles of boards, always keeping us right on surf etiquette.

Lisa once collared myself, Tom and Kev on the beach.

She kept going on about "you have to be flexible to surf well."

We all attempted to demonstrate our flexibility. Stretching from side to side, bending backwards.

Lisa started laughing "is that the best you can do?" she then executed a perfect cartwheel, straight into the splits.

With a few "fuck offs", we kicked sand at her.

"We aren't built to do that type of stuff", as we kicked more sand and retired to the pub.

I'm sure she still laughs at our pathetic attempts still.

If there was any surf at all, we would be in there. In all conditions from the small sloppy waves to the giant storm monsters.

It was a harsh apprenticeship but it helped us build up surf fitness and knowledge.

I loved being propelled beachwards at great speed but wanted to progress. Paddling had now become second nature to us all, hard work but worth it. Our one goal to get out back, where the waves were just thinking of breaking.

We all had our own ways of getting through the waves, the duck dive, the eskimo roll and the chuck your board into the face of the wave. We all got there eventually.

Our work was paying dividends, but we still took a lot of poundings from the unforgiving sea.

We soon sussed out that at certain times of tide, if you walked a few hundred yards to the river mouth then the paddle out wasn't as bad.

As our surfing was starting to improve, Tom suggested shooting the pier. Riding through the large pier legs avoiding the metalwork. It seemed easy enough but in practice it was a nightmare.

The trick was to get plenty of speed off the face of the wave, duck and hopefully shoot through to the other side.

After a couple of collisions, I managed to get half way through.

With the board sinking I was hit by another wave, dragged backwards. I was trapped either side of a pier leg, my leash wrapped around.

Luckily I managed to pull the velcro apart and escape with the board only slightly scarred.

Tom got the knack of it after a few near misses.

Jeff wasn't so lucky.

On the biggest wave of the day, he went for the pier shoot, wipedout, slamming into the pier leg. You can still see the dent.

For his troubles he got a broken jaw and a very apt nickname "Dangerous" Jeff.

Tash put up with a lot of stick from us. He could hardly swim but with his board his confidence really started to grow.

He did have the odd moan about the temperature of the water, sewage, the price of beer, people in wheelchairs crossing roads, well about everything really but that's Tash.

After spending too much money hiring gear from Nick and Gary's famous surf van, I decided that it was time to get my own gear.

I had seen a couple of lads in homemade wetsuits. It was a cheap option but fraught with danger as it required some skill cutting out and bonding together. I thought it best to get a ready made wetsuit, one that actually fit.

Dangerous Jeff went for the bright look orange and red wetsuit, we wouldn't loose him in a hurry.

Tom, Tash and Ste went for more sedate darker colours.

I saved up and bought a Typhoon wetsuit from Dennys dive shop in Redcar.

It was a winter suit 6, 4 and 3mm thick, coloured black and blue (very apt).

It was a brilliant suit, keeping you warm on the coldest days. It allowed you to have a longer time in the water.

Old ladies would come over to us, in the carpark or on the beach, after watching us from the pier and say "eee you must be freezing in that sea."
We would just smile take our wetsuits off halfway and steam in front of them.
I think they just did it for a bit of a perve.

As it was getting towards Winter, I bought boots and gloves from the van. Pure indulgent luxury.

After getting too many ice-cream heads, (having your head frozen by the seawater, giving blinding flashes and headaches that you wouldn't believe), I bought a hood.

A tight fitting balaclava that protected you from the cold but also made you look a right dickhead.

I never got used to the restrictiveness of the hood and it was soon consigned to the back of the garage, roll on the ice-cream heads.

Plenty of people wear these, some wear them through the summer, each to their own.

Everyone I met was mesmerised by the varying form of the waves, hypnotised by the rhythmic beauty of the sea.

We all developed a "surfers stare", a place where you can loose yourself quite easily. Through wave watching, you learnt a lot. Where the waves were breaking best, at what state of tide and where the sandbars were.

That Winter, I learned one of the great secrets of cold water surfing.
Pissing in your wetsuit.
Yes, as you enter the cold North sea, pee in your wetsuit.
This puts an initial warm layer around you.
I know it sounds a bit disgusting but don't knock it until you've tried it.
Another thing I learned, was to always wash my wetsuit out in fresh water to get rid of the seawater and urine smell.
Some of the lads didn't bother, their suits stank and soon dropped to pieces.

At the time, a couple of the lads couldn't afford gloves, so they tried various other options to keep their hands warm.
Socks were tried but didn't really work, they did give us a good laugh though.
Marigold gloves tucked into wetsuit sleeves, was only slightly more effective but the piss taking was worse than suffering cold hands. Especially when the pink ones came out.
Cold frostbitten fingers, joints that you couldn't move were just a couple of hardships we had to endure.

I was in desperate need of a board of my own.

In the surf shop, they had all the latest boards Local motion, Wave Graffiti, T & C, Free Spirit (which were superbly crafted in Whitby by Sedge), Laser, Ocean magic and many other quality boards but they all seemed very short, aimed at the more experienced rider.

I scanned the local paper, the Evening Gazette, as well as the free paper for a suitable board, not really knowing what I was looking for.

One night, I spotted an advert for a second hand board, a 6 foot 6", it said it was in good condition.

It was a bit shorter than I would have liked but the price swung it, only £50.

I went round for a look.

It was bright orange with a lightening bolt on the deck, it looked O.K. and it came with a leash.

I handed over the money and was stoked to have a board of my own.

Later I realised that I should have waited but at the time all I wanted was a board of my own.

Others had also invested in a variety of boards, some battered, some brand new.

It wasn't long before I got it in the water at Saltburn.

On a day when there were good moderate sized waves, being held up by a light offshore wind, I paddled out back behind the breaking waves.

I waited for a bigger set to come through, as I'd seen the proper surfers do.

I picked my wave.

Letting the first in a set of 3 roll past, I then paddled as hard and as fast as I could.

For a split second I looked back just as the wave broke.

Off balance and in the wrong place I was tumbled by the wave and wiped out.

Seconds later I paddled back out into position and waited to try again.

Another set wasn't far away, I paddled, felt the power of the wave push me forward towards the beach.

The sun came out, blinding me, I got to my feet.

It wasn't pretty, elegant or very steady but I was riding the wave.

I couldn't believe it, I turned the board one way then the other, it responded well.

It wasn't slashing cutbacks, it was just steady away.

Just as I was getting used to being on my feet riding a wave, the power ebbed from the wave on the board sank.

I gave a loud "yeeeeehaaaa", I was buzzing and no-one had even noticed.

I tried again and again, the wipeouts came thick and fast.

Bambis first steps came to mind.

Every wave I learned a bit more, it was going to be a long, long learning curve. A lifetime in fact.

In those early weeks on the Tango board, I did crash into the pier.

It left a 6" scar on the deck, which I fixed with pink resin which I had found in the garage. Not pretty but effective.

We rode more and more waves. A crowded day at Saltburn, meant around 20 surfers in the water.

On a good day, we would surf for a few hours, come out, have something to eat then hit the surf again.

Out for more food then back into the surf again.

We surfed up to 12 hours a day.

Knackered, we always ended up in Rosies for a few beers.

There's really nothing better than to chill out with good friends, listen to good music, talking complete shite, watching the waves and get slowly hammered.

Safe in the knowledge that you are going to be doing the same thing again tomorrow.

As you can tell, we did this a lot.

On one very clean 4 foot day, with light offshore wind blowing, I paddled from the rivermouth over to Penny's hole, as I could see it was beginning to work well.

It was one of those quiet moments that you sometimes get, when the world seems to stop and everything is calm. A time when you find your surfing soul.

I sat on my board watching for a set to come.

I then had a strange feeling, like I was being watched.

A couple of lads were at the rivermouth, others nearer to the pier but no-one close by.

Maybe I'd drank too much the night before?

I waited.

The dark shadow of a set started to roll in.

I turned to paddle for the first wave and stopped dead in the water.

10 feet away, right in front of me, an inky black head stared at me.

Large black, unblinking eyes focused on me.

To say that I shit myself, was an understatement.

I looked, it looked.

I thought about shouting for help but everyone was too far away.

The wave passed by.

I sat watching the huge seal.

The seal stared back.

The thought "did it fancy me?" crossed my mind.

Thankfully I don't think I was its type.

As quickly and as silently as it arrived, it disappeared.

I caught the next wave in.

When I started to tell people, it turned out that the seal and its friends were regular visitors to Saltburn.

I have seen them since but never as close as the first time.

Nature has a wonderful knack of giving us all wake up calls.

Sometimes you have to look really closely, other times you just get slapped in the face.

As new swells arrived, we would drive up and down the coast looking for the best spot.

Gallons of petrol were usually wasted, as a procession of cars and vans toured all the usual suspect breaks.

Everyone usually ended back in Saltburn.

It did get a bit annoying at times, you'd driven over 20 miles and found a smaller wave than you had left.

Many of us were the "get in while you can" school, others though were looking for the perfect wave and remained frustrated all day.

We would pass each other, heading in different directions.

Windows were wound down "S'lands cranking, it's really going off", they would speed off only to find a gutless 2 foot wave.

Sometimes you could hear the shouts "bastaaarrrrddddsssss."

At this point, I feel that I should give you a very brief bit about the history of Saltburn.

Basically it is a small town in the North East of England, famous for being an Edwardian / Victorian holiday destination, made popular by Henry Pease who spent a lot of time and money getting Saltburn right.

It has a long history of smuggling and is part of Captain Cook country. Cooks Dad is buried in Marske, very close to a very good surf spot.

I'm sure you know of his 3 famous voyages and how he and his crew witnessed Hawaiian chiefs riding the waves, on shaped wooden boards.

It seems like a bit of a coincidence that years later we are doing the same thing.

I was told that surfing at Saltburn started in the 60's, but maybe Cook or one of his crew started here much earlier!

The Victorians could stroll down Marine parade; take the Cliff lift or the steps down to the bottom of the bank. Take tea in the Valley gardens, or gaze upon towering Huntcliff.

The Victorians, in their wisdom, built a pier.

Little did they know year's later, surfers who were too lazy or who couldn't paddle out would launch themselves off the end.

Saltburn was a Quaker village. That mentality hung around for years, no official pubs just hotels with bars.

On the practical side of Saltburn life and most importantly are obviously the pubs.

Rosie O' Grady's (Bankside, now Vista Mar) was always a good place to meet. It is only a short stagger away from the car park and an ideal place to watch the surf.

The Marine is a strange old place that never really changes. Friday and Saturday nights were always good. When we first started to go there it was classed as a sports club and you had to produce your card to get in.

The back Alex, Queens (now Windsor's), and the Vic were the other pubs we mostly frequented. The ship was a bit more traditional, a smugglers haven. A good place to kick back.

I will get to Philmores nightclub, the best club in the world, in a few chapters, it's worth the wait.

Back to it.

We had started to meet more and more surfers. People like Mal Meadows, Tilly, Willy, Teacher John, College Chris, Phil the Dil, Solicitor Graham, Capetown Ken (the knee boarder), Matty and Jeff "Riddler" Ridley.

Donkey Al (he used to be a jockey but didn't ride many winners), and Mickey Prouse were 2 surfing characters who were mad in or out of the water.

They would try to ride into each other.

If one got a wave, the other would follow and run the other over. Donk had a powerful slashing style on his short board; Prousey rode a battered green longboard, twice the width of mine.

Prousey would catch a wave, lay down on his board, arms folded across his chest and ride it all the way to the beach. The King of the coffin ride.

I met Keldy at work; he was based in the same steel mill about ¾ of a mile away.

You always knew when he was on shift, as the smell of his simmering curry's filtered out from the mechies workshop.

He'd been surfing for a while and had been to Sri Lanka a couple of times.

He had a white VW van and was in the process of kitting it out, ideal for the surfing life.

People loaned us now classic videos, Endless summer, Crystal voyager, Beyond blazing boards, Free ride, Morning of the earth and many others.

We watched Lance Carson, Greg Noll, Buttons, Nat Young, Rabbit, PT, Occy, Rell Sun, Gerry Lopez and so many others. They all were to become the best role models in the world the only thing was none of them wore 6mm wetsuits and surfed in sewage.

We watched the long range weather forecast on the BBC, Thursday nights and farming outlook for a more in-depth view. We learned how to decipher the weather charts in the papers.

We knew when a new groundswell was coming and we'd be ready.

We even listened into the shipping forecast at unearthly hours on the radio.

Everyone we talked to seemed to suggest that we needed to broaden our surfing horizons, a surf safari was needed.

We narrowed it down to Thurso at the top of Scotland, with its famous breaks of Brims Ness and Thurso East or Newquay at the other end of the country.

It was a hard decision, both about the same distance away but Newquay "surf city" won the day with the promise of warm weather and surf.

FIRST TRIP TO NEWQUAY

We had read all the magazines and heard the stories about "Surf city", it was time to see for ourselves what the British capital of surfing was really like.

We discussed the trip for a while, general pub talk...nothing happened.

Out of the blue, the Newquay trip sprang into life, everyone seemed up for it.

It was early Spring and the thought of surfing all the mythical breaks and in warmer water, was an exciting prospect.

We were ready...well almost.

We hired a blue ford van to take us the 400 miles down to Newquay.

Myself, Tom, Kev, Tash, Ste and Dod packed the van. Wetsuits, boards and lots of lager went in.

We had booked a static caravan for the week, just outside of Newquay, handy for the beaches and pubs.

The journey down is still a bit of a blur, as we were all in party mode.

We lasted a full 5 minutes before the first can of lager was cracked open, on the Parkway (A174).

We had quite a few piss stops along the way.

Tom was the elected driver, obviously drawing the short straw.

He didn't seem to mind too much.

About 9 hours from home, we arrived in Newquay.

It was quite magical, it felt like we were aboard. Palm trees were growing in peoples front gardens, the sun was out, everyone was walking around in shorts and T-shirts.

VW campers lined every street and every car had a board on its roof.

You could feel that the whole place was very chilled out.

We found the caravan site after a few detours, around the town and down country lanes.

The woman who checked us in, looked us all up and down, gave us the key and sent us on our way.

Dod dived into the caravan and claimed the double bed.

Myself and Kev got the kitchen table, that turned into a double bed. Tom, Ste and Tash were left in the lounge area.

With sleeping arrangements sorted, we followed the signs to Fistral beach.

This is what we had travelled hundreds of miles for and we weren't disappointed. A 3-4 foot wave was breaking as we drove up the bank, past the golf course, towards the Headland hotel and then down to the beach carpark.

For a few minutes, we all stood and watched the turquoise waves break with such consistency.

Even the white water was, well, white!

100 people were in the water but it didn't look crowded.

The beach was filled with people setting up for the day.

Windbreaks, towels, bucket and spades, picnics, you get the picture.

We changed quickly and surfed or attempted to surf in the warm water for hours.

No gloves needed, happy days.

The wipeouts kept on coming but so did the longer rides.

Later in the session we all had a few close encounters with the rocks, at the base of the Headland, all managed to survive.

Everyone apart from Kev returned to the van.

After 40 minutes there was still no sign of him.

We knew that he had been near the rocks with us, we all scanned the waves.

We eventually spotted him walking back from the other end of the beach, when he got back he explained that he had moved away from the rocks but got caught in a rip and taken to the other end of Fistral.

Over the next few days we surfed every break possible. Perrenporth, Fistral, Towan, Great Western and last but not least Tolcarne. I'll get to that in a bit.

Our first night we ordered a taxi for 6, to go from the campsite into Newquay. We all expected a minibus but a proper limo appeared.

I realise you see them everywhere now but then it was a rare sight.

We got in and told the driver to take us "where the pubs are."

As we drove a young female voice, silky smooth, came over the radio in the limo.

"Bet she's a bit of a go-er" one of us said.

"Yes she is", the limo driver replied, "that's my wife."

After a short pause, we pissed ourselves laughing. We booked the limo every night and had a really good laugh with him.

In Newquay itself, we did a tour of the pubs. The Sailors, Red Lion, Central, Newquay arms and then back again. We sampled Newquay steam for the first time, not bad.

It was early in the tourist season but there were still plenty of people out and about. We finished off at the pizza shop near the Red Lion, everything with garlic.

Back at the caravan we downed more cans of lager, eventually crashing in the early hours.

"Psssst", I was woken by the sound of cans of lager being cracked open.

Ste greeted me with "Morning, want some breakfast" he then thrust a can into my hand.

He went around everyone and did the same thing.

He then sat himself down in front of the telly, can in hand, with a big grin on his face. Happy that he'd made everyone breakfast.

Later that morning , 5 very fit lasses turned up at the campsite. They began to put their tent up opposite.

We all piled out, drooling.

"Do you want a hand?" Tash shouted.

"If you don't mind" came the reply.

We all stood and applauded.

They didn't get it.

A couple of minutes later, myself and Kev walked over and uttered the classic line.

"Do you fancy a finger?"

We counted the seconds.

"What did you say?"

"Do you fancy a f-i-n-g-e-r" this time we said slower so they could understand.

The look on their faces was a picture. Sort of, stunned beyond belief followed by complete anger.

They all started coming towards us.

As we saw the whites of their eyes, out came the Cadburys chocolate fingers, from behind our backs.

Yes they did still come over and batter us but it was a good way to break the ice.

They turned out to be from Dorset and up for a party.

We had a couple of cracking nights with them, partying long into the night.

After another mad night around Newquay, Dod threw, what can only be called, a bit of a wobbler.

He has a very strong character, was pissed and got slightly upset over something.

It ended up with the kitchen bed in pieces, smashed cups and Dod locked out of the caravan naked.

After he had calmed down we let him back in.

We all made up and did a reconstruction job on the bed.

The week was going in far too quickly but we tried to pack as much in as possible.

On one of the last mornings, we woke up early put the gas fire on and watched Winnie the Pooh, in the blustery day on television.

We watched it as no-one had the energy levels to change the channel over.

Either that or we were doing really good student impressions.

Eventually, we all got up and checked Fistral out.

It was starting to turn big and nasty, storm swell waves were starting to roll in.
We decided for a look at Tolcane, as we hadn't surfed there yet.

It didn't look too bad from the top of the cliffs, 4 of us got changed ready for battle.

Dod and Ste decided to take a few photos and go to the pub.

At beach level, it was a mass of whiter water, a very mean shore break with the promise of big storm waves, if we could make it out back.

Giant walls of water rolled in.

We were young, naïve but determined.

We were in no mood to back down from anything, let alone a bit of white water.

Myself, Tom, Kev and Tash began the long paddle against the never ending pounding waves.

Usually, there's a lull between sets but the waves on this day just kept coming.

We were getting full on storm waves, hammering in at us.

Just when our energy levels were getting low, we made it out back.

We sat on our boards, giving thumbs up to each other.

You couldn't help but notice a ship, the Ross Alcedo, very close to us and the shore.

A larger set came in, Tom paddled further out and caught it.

The rest of us, who thought we were out back we proved wrong.

We were sucked in and spat out, pounded and tumbled.

This certainly wasn't a fun session.

I caught a glimpse of Dod and Ste on the beach, pointing and laughing.

Bastards.

Another large set loomed.

We lasted less than a couple of hours, battered and bruised we retired to the nearest pub and got hammered again.

The next day on the local news we saw the Ross Alcedo again. Its engines had lost power and was now stranded on Tolcane beach.

Kev chipped in with "Fucking hell, we could have been squashed by that big boat."

We knew he was right.

Throughout the week we had walked around all the surf shops. Admired the boards, wetsuits, everything really.

We were seduced by names like Mambo, Quicksilver, Billabong, Mystic knights of Bali, Rip curl, Gotcha etc.

We bought Fat Willy's, surf rats and cats T-shirts.

We bought everything. Brighter the better.

We hadn't got a clue.

We even bought bright orange zinc sun block.

What complete dicks we must have looked, sat out back at Fistral on a gloomy day.

Young and stupid.

On the second last night, sat in a pub, we decided to have a competition to bring back the most unusual item back to the caravan.

It seemed like a good idea at the time and everyone was up for it. When your full of beer common sense goes out the window.

Back at the caravan we amassed;-

The only menu from our favourite pizza shop,

A matching toilet and sink,

A durex machine,

A plug from a swimming pool, (I kid you not),

Plus various other bits and pieces of contraband.

The competition was called a draw, we toasted our madness and then dumped all the gear out of the way around the back of the caravan.

Next morning we were woken by a group of lads being evicted from a caravan nearby.

As we watched we realised that it should have been us.

With pleas of "it wasn't us" and "we didn't take the fucking toilet and sink" .

They were thrown off the site.

The guilt lasted a couple of minutes then we had a bloody good laugh about it.

We had a really good time in Newquay, it was a wrench to leave. The trip home was quiet and subdued everyone totally knackered.

In our brief conversations, we all agreed that we would be back.

GIANT LEAPS

One unusually sunny but flat day down in Saltburn carpark, I got talking to Jeff Ridley about all things surfing.

Jeff had a million and one surfing stories and was keen to pass them on.

He talked about longboards, styles, soul surfing, the spirit of surfing and about waves.

We sat in his red and white 1963 split screen van, a true classic surf van. A van that put a smile on everyone's face. I got the grand tour of the stunning van.

I started to saying that I loved the van and would I like to have one.

Then the bombshell hit.

Jeff said "Well I'm selling her, do you want to buy it?"

Of course I wanted to buy it but being skint at the time, I had to decline the offer.

Gutted.

I did know Tom was looking around for a van, so I did a bit of matchmaking and Tom ended up buying it.

Tom was over the moon with it. Being a very good friend, he let me leave my stuff in it and let me stop whenever I wanted.

This meant that we could spend longer, living and sleeping surfing.

At this point, in my surfing life, I have to say that I still ventured home for showers and a change of clothes. Others didn't.

As you can imagine some of the cars and vans became very gungy, more "spunk pits."

My surfing outlook was changing, my direction clear.

I wanted to ride with the wave and be on it for as long as possible. Not slashing at the face of a wave for 2 seconds.

Riding a longboard and having a laugh with a few friends was the way to go.

A lot of lads persisted with shortboards but longboarding was the future for me.

I had seen the light.

On a Summers evening, in the Middle house pub in Marske, myself and Tom sat with our new Fat Willy's sweatshirts on. Obviously trying to impress the barmaids.

We were approached by 2 slightly younger lads, who had had a few.

They sat down with us and started asking all sorts of questions.

"Are you pseudo surfers?"

"Have you ever seen a fucking surfboard?"

This wasn't going to end well. I kept hold of my Newcastle brown bottle just in case it kicked off.

They had both had a lot more to drink than us and they were starting to get more aggressive.

Just as I thought, here we go.

We managed to get a word in. We managed to explain to them that we'd been surfing at Saltburn for a few months and that we had been to Newquay.

Tom mentioned that knew Nick and Gary.

Within seconds their attitude changed.

We had just met Kev Elliot and A the B (Anth the Bastard), a sort of good cop bad cop duo.

Apparently they had been surfing for a while but our paths had never crossed. We got on like a house on fire, after the initial stutter. More like minded people.

That weekend, we met Anth and Kev, they introduced us to Shorty and Leggy, two younger lads with far too much energy, superb surfers and true characters. We also met Big Neil, a quiet giant.

These were surfers that we'd said hello to but that was it. Now we were about to get to know them better.

Only small surf forced us into a marathon drinking session. Rosies, the Marine and then onto Philmores.

The party continued on the beach around a massive bonfire, the first of many.

PHILMORES

Just a short bit about Philmores nightclub. It was located 100 yards away from the carpark, ideal for everyone.

I had been going there for years and only realised later, that it was the best nightclub in the world.

In our area there were other clubs we'd go to.

The Top Deck, Revelles, Silks, The Madison and Club M but Philmores was local and you always had a good laugh there.

In the early days, the lasses would drink cherry B, rum / pernod and black, diesel or snake bites, very cosmopolitan. The lads stuck to lager.

Everyone would have their best gear on, the lasses must have spent days on their hair with the curling tongs.

Different bands would come to entertain.

Edwin Starr, was a favourite of mine, represented soul, Eek a mouse, reggae, there were lots of disco artists and rave groups / MCs / DJs (including the Rebel MC). Bernard Manning even showed up.

At the big black entrance doors, everyone lied about their age. Avoiding eye contact with the bouncer, you would pay the entrance money, maybe get a cloakroom ticket and then you'd be in.

I first went when I was 14 and I did look young.

My sister needed someone to go with, she was meeting her mates inside.

I couldn't believe I got in, no-one batted an eye lid.

I was also gobsmacked, when my sister sent me to the bar, to get drinks for her and her mates.

I got served, no questions asked.

Philmores went through a lot of changes over the years. Every now and again it burnt down but always, phoenix like, rose from the ashes.

The dance floor was surrounded by booths (ideal for snogging), neon lights which filled the walls and an old car that was parked in a corner (didn't really get that).

One thing that never, ever change was the sticky carpets. It was easy to loose a shoe on the treacle like flooring.

During the Winter months, getting some food, gave a new meaning to danger.

First you had to scale the bank, usually covered by a very slippy sheet of ice.

If one fell, you all fell, it was complete chaos at times.

Once at the top of the bank, it depended on how pissed you were, if you were going to risk getting food from the toxic burger van. Famous worldwide for the fluorescent peas.

Buses waited at the top of the bank to either go to Marske and Redcar or Skelton, Brotton and Guisborough. No matter how drunk you were, it was very important to get on the right bus.

People who got on the wrong bus were never seen again.

Philmores attracted people from all over the local area.

Thursdays, was student or birthday night, Fridays and Saturdays was always packed.

It might have been the beer but it always felt like lasses were in the majority and up for anything.

In a group the experience got better. "Come on Eileen" still reminds me of the circle of high kicking friends and strangers. Dancing and singing the wrong words.

There were fights but the bouncers usually sorted everything out.

We all knew if you got caught fighting you got thrown out, no messing.

The rave scene seemed to happen over night, Philmores was transformed. Turning from a good local nightclub, into something really special.

Coaches started arriving from Manchester, Liverpool and London, something was happening.

The first time I noticed the dramatic change was on an Autumn night.

We'd been surfing all day and now the party was well on the way.

On Entering the club, a wall of sound nearly knocked you off your feet, the floor was bouncing.

On the way to the bar complete strangers were hugging and kissing us.

"What the hell is going on?", I shouted, no-one heard.

We went to the bar.

"4 CANS OF RED STRIPE"

The lass behind the bar shouted back "ARE YOU SURE?"

That threw me a bit "YESSSS, 4 RED STRIPE." I held up 4 fingers to help the lass.

She shrugged her shoulders and gave us a strange look.

I scanned the dance floor, it was a sea of bodies, dancing, bouncing as one. I looked around, everyone was drinking water.

"What the fuuuucckkks going on?"

I downed my can and launched myself into the middle of the dance floor, hands in the air, carried away by the madness.

The rave years stopped any fighting, everyone was so loved up, the bouncers were just for decoration.

People were off their heads, dancing, hugging and kissing.

Shirts came off lads and lasses as the night literally heated up.

Girls would walk up to us and ask for Vic to be rubbed onto their chests?!

Who were we to refuse.

'The walls drip with sweat in this Teesside club where bar staff sell water at 30p a half to Ecstasy kids'

If you wanted drugs then you were spoilt for choice.

Speed, ecstasy and cocaine were the preferred drugs at the time and were freely available. People were filling their boots.

As the months went by, the water in the gents toilets were switched off, the walls dripped like a sauna.

The price of water from the bar tripled.

No-one truly realized that this was a very special time but all good things come to an end.

There were rumors of Manchester drug dealers turning up with guns and threatening people. Don't know if that's true, they could have been from anywhere.

After another surf session, we went up to Rosie's. Shorty, Leggy and A the B were in the corner with a few people I didn't recognize. Myself, Tash and Tom got our beer and sat down with them.

We all exchanged the usual pleasantries, "alright, how you doing, that was a brilliant session."

We rattled on about the waves for a while and then one lad said "so do you know where to score, mate?"

"If you go to Philmores tonight you'll have no problems scoring."

"Yeah, were playing there tonight,"

"aye right! you fucking Oceanic then?"

"Yeah."

It wasn't really clear if they were just bullshitting or not but we treated them like everyone else we met.

Had a laugh and took the piss.

Oceanic had the Insanity single out at the time, everyone was going mad for it.

We went up to a packed Philmores and watched them play. The place went off its tits.

WPC wearing swimsuit

'Dressed like that I did not feel out of place'

AN undercover policewoman described how she wore a swimming costume to attend a Rave Night at Philmore's nightclub.

WPC Susan Gaunt said she was sent to monitor activities inside the club.

"Dress in the club was always very casual," she said. "I wore a swimming costume and shirt, jeans and trainers.

Leggings

"On another occasion I wore a swimming costume and leggings. Dressed like that I didn't feel out of place."

She described how she saw two men drinking from the taps in the ladies toilets.

"Nobody objected to men being in there," she added.

Any dealers had a captive audience at a nightclub like Philmore's, according to a drug squad officer.

DC Terrence Waterfield described the street value of drugs to the magistrates.

People would pay up to £25 for Ecstasy, £7.50 for enough cannabis resin to make about 20 cigarettes, £5 for an Acid tablet and a gramme of amphetamine sulphate — known as a wrap — normally sold for about £10.

Mix

He explained that when taking such drugs people usually didn't drink alcohol as well.

"Since Ecstasy came into this area, and it isn't all that long ago, people don't normally mix it with alcohol because of the dehydration affect," he said.

"They go to places like Philmore's because these are the places where they know drugs are freely available.

"Drug dealers have a captive audience and there are many dealers around. There are places in this area where it is accepted that you can obtain drugs should you require them, and Philmore's nightclub is one of them."

Undercover police would show up every now and then. Most were easily sussed out. All with clubbing gear but all with highly polished shoes.

It was only a matter of time before the club was closed down. Everyone thought it would only be temporary.

We were wrong.

It's now the Spa hotel and restaurant, not quite the same.

Every now and again though Jason Busby, the mastermind of Big Beat which created such a stir, organizes a reunion which relives the Philmores experience from back in the day.

The party's over

THE PARTY'S over at a Cleveland rave venue following a court battle to have it shut down.

Magistrates have refused to renew the liquor licence for Philmore's in Saltburn after hearing claims that Ecstasy, LSD, amphetamines and cannabis were openly sold and used at the club.

Decision

Licensee Christopher Farrell was "not a fit and proper person" to hold a justices licence and the premises had not been "properly supervised", it was ruled.

The decision has pulled the plug on one of Cleveland's most popular nightspots, leaving many of the county's clubbers and those from further afield without their favourite venue.

The existing liquor licence for Philmore's only runs until April 4 And

● Caroline Llewellyn: 'Police saw drugs openly sold'

Club closed down

police are also objecting to the renewal of the club's entertainment licence, due to expire on the same date.

One senior police officer who visited a rave night at Philmore's alleged that drug-taking youngsters "weren't on this planet."

Force solicitor Caroline Llewellyn said undercover police had seen drugs being openly sold and used on 14 visits to the club.

Explaining Cleveland Police's objection to the renewal of the liquor licence, Mrs Llewellyn said closure was the only way to eradicate the club's reputation for drugs.

But Kenneth Brown, boss of club licence holders Kenbro Leisure Limited, claimed police had been

"hell bent" on closing Philmore's.

Solicitor Richard Hall, representing Kenbro Leisure, said the situation had been "grossly exaggerated" by the police.

Evidence

And a succession of clubgoers and Philmore's staff gave evidence claiming they had never seen drug dealing going on in the club.

However, hopes that the club would "rave on" were dashed when Langbaurgh East Licensing Justices, sitting at Guisborough magistrates on Saturday, refused to renew the liquor licence.

Following the ruling — reached on the fourth day of the hearing — a notice of appeal was served on the magistrates by Mr Hall. He said

One of the funniest nights was seeing Tom's youngest brother, Peter, trying to dance.

Two left feet didn't come close to it. Someone gave him something and he turned into the best dancer in the world.

After 3 hours non-stop we dragged him off the dance floor and gave him water. He said he felt fine but couldn't stop. He kept going for hours after and then crashed out big time.

Over the years Philmores was responsible for many relationships, some even ending in marriage. It was always a good place to go and meet like minded people.

It was a dark day when it was shutdown, but the escalating drug problem left the local council / police with no choice. It is sadly missed.

…back at the bonfire.

I nipped into the public toilets to be greeted by a lad called Rat, who was humping a lass from the nightclub. She was bent over the sink, spewing and making some alarming noises.

I wasn't sure if it was pleasure or pain.

We started a bit of a conversation,

"Alright, how's it going?" I said,

"Can't complain" Rat said, as he banged away.

"Are you two coming down to the fire?"

"Might be down after we've finished",

Rat pointed at the lass "Do you want a go?"

"Err, no not this time."

As I walked out the lass spewed some more, everywhere. It wasn't pretty.

After sitting around another fire, a daft lad called Milner suggested a nude surf.

It was 4 in the morning, we are all wasted and we are sat out back on our boards.

You couldn't see the waves you just had to listen out for them.

It was weird, sat in the dark watching the fire from the sea. We all caught a couple of waves before hypothermia set in.

It's amazing how fast you can sober up, when your bollock naked paddling about, with the odd wave breaking over you.

It's only then that you realise that you must be slightly mad.

Lads and lasses, stood clapping and cheering, as we were getting out. They were obviously having a good time, as they all had massive Bob Marley joints.

A car pulled into the carpark, it cruised up.

A police car stopped.

Two policemen opened their windows and said "everything O.K. lads?"

53

What could we say?

We were cold, naked and only had our boards covering our vital bits. Others continued to smoke.

We all smiled.

They shook their heads, laughing and drove away.

Good community policing.

This set the trend for years to come. Surf, drink, drugs and sex.

Usually accompanied with a fire on the beach.

We got quite organised. Well organised chaos.

Tom acquired a 45 gallon oil drum, cut it in half and made a stand for it.

We filled it with BBQ coals and used and abused it for years.

Luckily, one of the lads worked in the local butchers so we were never short of meat.

There wasn't many vegetarians about then.

People used to turn up with vans busting at the seams, full of wood for the beach fires.

We never ran short.

At the time drugs were unbelievably easy to come by, a lot of my friends and acquaintances enjoyed smoking ganja, (marijuana).

I wasn't that bothered, as a non-smoker, so I got pissed instead.

There was a lot of experimentation going on.

Different people mixed some drugs, others mixed them all. Some partied their way through it without any side affects. Others didn't cope well.

Magic mushrooms were always a natural alternative, they usually got made into a tea or soup.

One of the lads was chased around by a giant beach ball, people stopped and stared as he shouted "It's going to eat me, the balls going to eat meeeeeee."

Another one of the lads seemed fine watching the clouds go by, then he disappeared.

He was later found in the toilets on his hands and knees, searching for his cock in the urinals. He was convinced that it had dropped off... funny things these drugs, even the natural ones.

We met more and more surfers. Wils, Big Si, Karl "Ledge" Frampton, Levi, Big Mike and Auds, Ozzie Ste and Andrea, Diamond Dave, Ando, Fraiser, Barry, Boyd, Lee, Ged, Turkey Mick, Archie and Irish Graham. All are really good people with a love of the sea.

Ozzie Ste was a "goatboater" or surf skier, when he first started. Working near Plate mill were always talked waves and surfing.

After months of barracking, he discovered surfing. Eventually seeing the light, getting himself a longboard.

A the B turned up one day with his mate Keith, who was in the Navy. They had surfed together for years.

I asked what he did in the Navy.

I got the nightclub reply, "I drive a nuclear submarine."

As a true sceptic I told him to "fuck off, that's bullshit."

He insisted that it was true. I shook my head in disbelief.

About 6 months later, News at 10 came on.

A special live report from the bridge of a nuclear sub.

Who got interviewed first...yep, the driver. Keith.

I fully expected the 2 fingered salute, followed by told you so, but it never came.

Keith turned up now and again, always in a fast car. Surfed for a while and then disappeared. The nature of his work I suppose.

As surfing families go we have one of the best.

Boyd, Barry and Fraiser not only surf well but all possess good business sense as well. Amusement arcade to clothes to cafes they're doing it all.

Wils and Big Si would usually turn up together. After a drink fuelled weekend Wils ended up on crutches, with a broken ankle.

Jumping out of a first story window isn't recommended.

While sat out back one day, a lad paddled out past me, he nodded and said "alright, its looking good."

Then he caught some cracking waves.

A group of us were going up to Rosies to start a marathon drinking session, we asked if he was coming.

As we downed the first couple of lagers, a waitress came up with a pot of tea and put it in front of Rossy, the man with the glasses.

We were stunned.

After a short silence and a few raised eyebrows, we started ripping into him.

"Are you a fucking college boy?",

"How gay are you!"

"Would you like some cake as well?"

Rossy was an easy target and we were on a roll.

Thankfully Paul took it in good part and soon became a cornerstone in our community, as well as a good friend.

As I got to know him, I found out that we shared a love of music and with Philmores so close dancing.

Many nights were spent stomping or souling out.

My Mam always asks "How's gay Paul doing?"
This is because he was wearing a bright shirt the first time she met him.

He once featured on World of Sport, the one with Dickie Davies. Not for drinking tea but for swimming. He nearly caused a big upset by pushing the British number one, at the time, all the way.

Mike and Auds were always around and with them was the very friendly dog, Cavell.
There was a bit of shouting from inside the van one day, Rossy came out, shouting "the dog's just bit me!"
He was right the dog had just bitten him.
What he didn't tell us was that, he'd just bitten the dogs ear!? Cos it was there.

The TV camera's for Heartbeat would turn up every now and again. They seemed to love the views of the beach and the pier.
What really pissed them off was having surfers, riding waves in the background. Many a filmed wave was consigned to the cutting room floor.

In Summertime the days were long and lazy. We surfed through the longest day, making an effort to be in the water as long as possible.
It never got truly dark, when the sun started to come up all of us were in.

The nightmare of putting on a cold wetsuit, soon faded, as a ball of bright orange greeted us for another day.

Wintertime was slightly different.
I think everyone hated the short days and limited surfing time.
We would cram into vans waiting for the wind or hail to stop. Pot noodles and cup a soups kept us going.
Life at the cutting edge of surfing wasn't easy.
The Winter swell's always came, waking us with a roar, powerful Northerly waves.
Freezing conditions and the difficult paddleout were forgotten as you took your first drop down a mountainous Winter wave.
The wipeouts didn't seem to matter, two or three cannonball rides hanging on and flying down the line, made everything worthwhile.

Philmores as I have mentioned was a good starting point for a good weekend.
With our surfing community basing itself in the carpark, in cars and vans, it couldn't have been better.
The beach parties really started to take off, word spread and at times it got a bit wild.
Lasses would turn up, some we knew, others we had seen in Philmores or in one of the pubs but some were complete strangers. They all seemed friendly and most didn't bite.
For some unknown reason, lasses seemed to like surfers.
Some were after love and long term relationships.
Others just wanted to shag your brains out.
I'm not sure if it was the laid back attitude or the fact that we were really handsome bastards (aye, right), or maybe it was because we always had booze and drugs nearby.
Who knows.

Many a shagging session took place in the carpark, under the pier, on the pier, on the beach and in the vans.
Everybody has many recollections about this time, most unprintable.
Girls would turn up ready to party, they would use and abuse us and be gone by morning.
In a few of the vans, knickers were taken as trophies.
This pastime didn't last long, as after a few weeks even in the gungiest van you could notice the smell.

It nearly knocked you over.
We ending up sacrificing them all on a large fire.
The fire burnt for days!

One near miss for myself, came after a long surf session.

I had changed and was in need of a few beers. Up the steps to Rosies and straight to the bar.

As I waited to be served I was surrounded by 2 very large lasses from Stockton. They were straight off the pages of Viz.

They must have been quite posh as all their tattoos were spelt right. You get the idea.

They started to ask questions;-

"Are you one of them surfers?"

"Do you live down there in the carpark?"

"Can we both come down and have a look?"

I took a mouthful of lager.

Then they both said "we've always wanted to shag a surfer." Squeezing my arse.

The lager was spat everywhere.

I could see the lads in the corner laughing their tits off.

I took the lasses over and we all sat down.

I asked if they knew where Cinderella was?

The ugly sisters didn't get it.

The lasses were in surfer heaven, they were grabbing everyone.

We had a few more drinks then one by one, slipped away and legged it up to the Marine.

A lucky escape.

Next morning I spotted the lasses, in the carpark.

They looked as though they had been dragged through a bush backwards, hair and clothes all over the place.

They were coming out of the pie mobile, one of the smallest vans.

They had obviously got what they had come for.

One Friday night, as we were drinking in the"surfers corner" in Rosie's, something strange happened.

A dozen of us had been drinking for a couple of hours, we had been joined by a few lasses which we had known for ages and 2 newcomers.

"Viking" Keith, out of the blue started to commentate on a nonexistent race.

"And the runners of todays race are coming down to the starting post..."

Most of us thought that he'd had a few too many or was just loosing his marbles.

Things got a bit more interesting when A the B and Rossy got up and started walking about.

"and there off...."

A the B and Rossy started jogging on the spot.

There were a few confused looks.

Keith continued with the commentary, the lads responded by jogging faster.

The 2 new lasses loved it and were clapping and cheering.

The 2 lads were running and jumping imaginary barriers.

Totally knackered, A the B was pronounced the winner.

Everyone clapped but didn't quite understand, until Keith pointed at one of Rosie's famous posters on the wall.

It read;-

Scarborough Fair

Two pigs to be ran for over a distance course.

Winner gets a pig and so does second place.

All comers welcome.

Keith pointed at the poster then the 2 lasses.

"There you go lads, there's the pigs for you."

The penny dropped, the lasses weren't impressed but the rest of us thought it was brilliant.

They did see the funny side after a few more drinks.

If someone was occupied in one van then we would just move to another or join in.

If someone turned up with a girl or girls then they were welcomed in.

One night I was trying to get to sleep in a top bunk.

One of the lads and his new acquaintance were making themselves comfortable below.

They were trying to be quiet but weren't succeeding.

There seemed to be a lot of fumbling around and then a whispered conversation started.

"Are you sure?"

"Try again", followed by more muffled noises.

"No, it still wont go, shit, I've never had this problem before."

The girl then said "well I've never done it before."

It took all my self control to keep the laughter in but they weren't finished.

"What are you kidding?"

"No, I've never done it before and I'm only 14.

Well at this point I couldn't help myself. I'd tried my best but couldn't hold back anymore, the full on belly laughs filled the van, tears filled my eyes.

The amorous couple left, pulling clothes on as they went.

To be honest she did look older but the school uniform was a bit of a giveaway.

Lasses would turn up on a regular basis, in ones or twos or they would bring all their sisters and would enjoy the company of a surfer or two.

Saltburn always seemed to be full of single lasses.

Rock chicks, students, tattooed women, fat women, thin women, crazy women and a lot of single mothers, all up for a laugh.

Relationships started to develop, some lasted a night, others a lot longer.

It wasn't unusual to see a lass out with different surfers in the same week.

All credit to the lasses who took up surfing, it can't have been easy entering the male dominated sport, at that time.

COMPETITIONS

I'm not really a competitive person, so competitions aren't really my thing.

I do however, think they are a good chance to meet up with old friends and new.

If you want to take things seriously then that's fair enough but if you want to have a party and a laugh then that's the time when we'd turn up.

As I have said, I am an average surfer who enjoys what I'm doing and I love riding on a longboard.

Saltburn competitions come around twice a year, Spring and Autumn.

Nick and Gary keep their infectious enthusiasm going not just for the more competitive surfers but for everyone.

They usually run 5 or 6 categories and put a lot of time and effort into the organization.

My competition debut started by mistake.

I had gone to check the surf out; an Autumn swell had started to come through and was breaking really nicely. A mellow 3 foot.

As I got changed, Ozzie Ste asked if I was going in the competition.

I started to say "I wasn't bothered and just wanted to surf."

Gary came out of the judge's caravan and convinced me to enter.

No-one had predicted surf so the competition entry wasn't the best.

With Gary and Nick judging and no-one else on a longboard, I surfed in the open competition against some really good surfers on toothpicks, sorry shortboards.

I enjoyed my time in the water, catching waves early and riding them all the way.

After the contest, I joined everybody at the presentation outside the caravan. I applauded as the winners, then Gary said "and the winner of the Autumn longboard competition is…"

I was very embarrassed, obviously getting it by default.

I was still chuffed to bits though.

It was yet another generous masterstroke by Nick and Gary, inspiring all the way.

The competitions at Saltburn drew in people from all over the country.

Word spread by word of mouth, phone calls and a bit of advanced warning in the surf magazines.

There were representatives from Tynemouth, South Shields, Hartlepool, Whitby, Scarborough, Blackpool, Manchester, Scotland etc.

In the early days, very few Southern surfers risked the journey North.

Maybe the sea was too cold or the thought of surfing in raw sewage put them off.

At this time, longboard riding in Saltburn exploded.

A small minority of shortboarders spat their dummies out. They claimed that we were catching all the waves.

They soon realized that they were talking bollocks and there was enough waves for everyone.

Peace was restored.

As well as Nick and Gary's competitions, Jeff Ridley came up with the East Coast Autumn Longboard Classic.

Yes it was a bit of a mouthful to say, but what an event.

Jeff aimed to promote the virtues of longboarding, the soul, the style and the camaraderie.

The event ran for 5 years through the 90's.

It started its life as a complementary event to Chapters Spring event in Devon.

Jeff soon put his own unique stamp on it.

AUTUMN 1991

Jeff called the contest on as the chart looked really good.

People arrived from all over Britain arrived, notably Johnny Kapec and Howard Davis.

Unfortunately, Michael Fish and his weather team had got it wrong. Instead of the hoped for 6 foot, we got no more than a 1 foot wave all weekend.

It was just about big enough to hold an expression session and have a laugh in the minimal surf.

A disappointing lack of surf was more than made up for by the surf do.

T shirts were raffled. Everyone got one, A the B ended up with 6.

Parky, ever the showman, was caught shagging in the toilets but that didn't seem to bother him.

The rest of us just went for it. Drinking and dancing late into the night.

AUTUMN 1992

This year the promised surf arrived, the surf gods were definitely smiling down on us.

A powerful 5 foot northerly swell greeted competitors from Northern Scotland, the North West and a good turnout from all the North East longboarders.

The heats were held over 30 minutes, so there were no excuses over paddling times. The best 3 waves counted.

There was a slight bit of controversy; one of the competitors was riding a short board. One that was shorter than 9 feet but in the spirit of the competition, he was allowed to continue as he was surfing so well.

I was in a heat with Gary and Tom, they were both on top form, brilliant. It was no surprise when I was knocked out.

At the end of the day, competitors were whittled down to 6 finalists for Sunday's grand finale.

We had the traditional surf do with "the band" taking centre stage.

Gary "Gannet" did a very individual version of Johnny B Goode, singing and mad dancing.

Everyone joined in and had a really good night.

Sunday morning, in the car park, a lot of sore heads were greeted by 6 foot perfection.

Corduroy lines, held up by offshore winds, created classic pure glass.

I gave Jeff a hand judging, with a couple of the other lads, from the portacabin next to the pier.

The 90 minute final was a complete mix of old and new styles.

Gary Rogers won the day with some inspirational riding.

He saved the best for last, getting tucked deep into a barrel, exploding out, cutting back and getting covered again. He finished off by walking to the nose of the board, hanging 10 for what seemed like an age.

It was a stunning ride, worthy of any competition.

All the finalists produced some stunning performances.

Nick Noble, surfed with a broken nose sustained in the heats, Rossy, Tom, Rick Bailey from Blackpool and teacher John Hukin. All deserved a medal for producing a stunning final.

Teacher John received a special trophy for the best wipeout. Another of Jeff's ideas.

The whole weekend was caught on film and was well covered in the local press.

The event had shown the virtues of longboarding, the soul, spirit, style and above all, the fun being shared with friends old and new.

A classic.

AUTUMN 1993

Surfers had gathered from far and wide, word had spread about the competition and everyone wanted to be part of it.

The car park filled with vans mainly VW and loads of cars.

Each and everyone had a longboard inside or strapped to the roof.

A heavy 6 to 8 foot swell pounded the coast. This wasn't going to be easy.

First timers to the competition included Ray from Manchester, with his very big dog. Mike from the RAF, whose wife had presented him with a longboard on their wedding day, weeks earlier. And Brian from Edinburgh, who had read articles from previous years in "Surf's up" magazine and made the effort to come down.

It was also a pleasant surprise to see dedicated short boarders take to longboarding with such enthusiasm.

Due to the difficult conditions, the heats were extended to 40 minutes. The paddle out was difficult even for the most experienced surfers.

Gary was once again surfing really well, until halfway through his heat, he body surfed into the beach. In the shore break he struggled to get out.

It turned out that he had broken his leg. He claimed the best wipeout prize for his troubles.

An ambulance quickly arrived and took Gary away to hospital. There were lots of concerned onlookers, some wanting a go of the gas and air!

Saturday night was a blast.

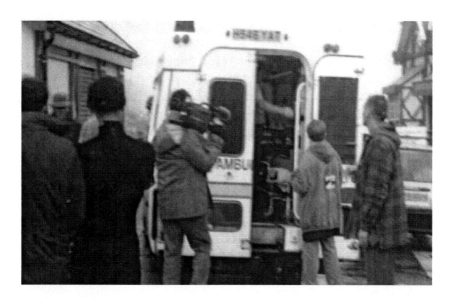

Sunday morning, people nursed hangovers and looked out on the cold and misty morning. Beautiful 5 foot waves peeling left and right. It was near perfect conditions.

In the final everyone again surfed well.

The honours went to Paul Ross who went "Off the Richter." His smooth soulful style, won a lot of admirers. He threw in some classic manoeuvres as well as some modern classics.

Rossy was followed home closely by Nick Noble, Tom, Rick Bailey, Teacher John and A the B.

It was another classic, Jeff had called everything right.

AUTUMN 1994

Jeff had been contacted by a large surf gear manufacturer; they had expressed a great interest in sponsoring the event.

With little time to go, they pulled out. This left Jeff in the proverbial.

Jeff wasn't in the best of health at the time and the event was unfortunately cancelled.

AUTUMN 1995

The swell came through, right on cue.

This year there were no distractions from this true grass roots event.

Jeff seemed to have a knack of calling the competition on, at the right time.

The heats were held in 3 − 4 foot waves, which frustratingly, dropped off throughout the day.

There were some really close heats and the judges had some difficult decisions to make.

Judging was being done from the end of the pier in heavy rain, testing conditions.

Next day conditions improved and a new powerful swell came through.

The semis were run off followed by a 45 minute final.

I had somehow managed to get through the heats and semi, I was now in the lion's den.

The surfing seemed to be of a high standard, as I watched my fellow finalists catch some brilliant waves.

My aim was to enjoy myself and have a few good rides of my own.

I earned the best wipeout award for a "shooting the pier" attempt, which went badly wrong.

The wave seemed to have enough power but died on me.

It left me in the middle of the pier with a set looming.

My leash parted company with my ankle and the board hit the pier.

It took a while to recover and I knew I was running out of time.

Gary claimed victory followed by Rossy, Nick, Tom, Mike "Bart" Smith and myself.

Another good year, surfed in difficult conditions.

AUTUMN 1996

Again the event was linked with a bit of a takeover, from the British Longboard Union (BLU), who were a part of the British surfing association. They wanted it to be part of a national tour, rumours of a £15, (a lot of money at the time, money that would be earmarked for beer), entrance fee got people talking.

Grass roots seemed to be giving way to big organizations and sponsorship. The East Coast Longboard Classic was meant to be an event where everyone could meet once a year, to celebrate Longboarding and to enjoy themselves. The competition was good but always secondary.

Jeff's idea of creating a gathering of longboard friends started to get lost. He called the competition off.

Sadly, the competition hasn't been run since. Jeff was suffering with ill health and moved away, eventually ending up in a remote Scottish island paradise.

All who took part or witnessed the events over the years will carry the memories for a very long time. Maybe The East Coast Longboard Classic will happen again. Who knows?

There have been many standout surfers at Saltburn throughout the years. Many have cut their surfing teeth in local competitions.

The Davies clan, from Tynemouth, would turn up on a regular basis. Peter, the Dad, Jessie, Gabe and Owain.

Sammy Lamiroy would also turn up around the same time and rip the place to bits.

These cheeky little kids were brilliant. You could tell early on, that these lads possessed an extraordinary talent.

That's not to say they had everything their own way, the local lads would always have something to say about that.

When we first started to surf, this Tynemouth lad turned up a couple of times.
He looked like a proper surfer, blond hair, tanned features.

I don't know what it was but there was something about him, a confidence, a look. He was just a normal daft Geordie lad.

It was only later that I found out that he was the one and only Nigel Veitch, a North East lad, who was on the ASP Pro tour. An inspiration / hero to many.

On one horrible rainy, grey day in the car park, Jeff came over to each van in turn and told us the news "Veitchy was dead."

Everyone was stunned. Small groups gathered, shocked.

How? Why? No way.

Later in the pub the atmosphere was quiet, we all listened to stories from people who had known him.

Competitions are usually completed over the weekend, surf permitting.

Friday night's are usually a good session spent in the pub with the odd person drinking cola.

Saturday's are spent having a bit of a surf do.

These shift venues on a regular basis. We've been to Rosie's, the Vic and on a couple occasions Rushpool hall.

We had a brilliant surf band, yes they were a bit rough around the edges but they would get everyone going and usually bring the house down.

Big Mike was the drummer, Shorty's brother Andy on guitar, Nick Noble also on guitar and the lovely Emma Bell vocals.

It's a shame they broke up, every time I saw them they were getting better and better.

Nowadays Nick has his own band, with Terry "the surfing fireman" and a few others.

It's slightly different music, professional and polished. Well worth anyone's trip up North.

Back to the competitions, Shorty had qualified for the Open final in Saltburn. He had been consistently surfing really well.

All the lads decided to celebrate this by partying all night ending up at Philmore's.

We finished off with pie and peas from the toxic burger van, at 3 in the morning.

Back down in the carpark, my sleeping bag was in Tom's van but he was occupied.

I borrowed Shorty's boardbag and crashed out in his van.

Very early morning, the sliding door of the van opened, Shorty threw up.

Fluorescent sick, thick bright green pea sick.

He kept spewing for 10 minutes. He was a mess, stinking of sick and whisky, still pissed.

After an hour of on / off sleep he did it again.

This time he even managed to spew down his T shirt.

A while later, Tom banged on the door, obviously full of beans.

"Are you'se getting up or what?"

He slid the door open and thought he'd stepped into a war zone.

"Oh god its stinks in here, what the hell were you drinking last night."

No time to answer, Tom said "and by the way the final starts in 5 minutes."

Shorty hid deep inside his sleeping bag and moaned "Just let me die."

Somehow between us we got him up, into his wetsuit and ready to go.

He looked like death warmed up and was still pissed.

We stuck his board under his arm and sent him on his way, just in time.

The hooter sounded and the 4 finalists entered the water.

We crossed our fingers Shorty would survive.

His first wave was a classic, a very slow knackered paddle, an attempt to stand followed by another. Up and riding he seemed to stumble, riding one footed, he then ducked into a small barrel, finishing off with and off the lip and a drunken dismount.

As we watched from the pier it became apparent that Shorty, even though not in full control, was having a brilliant session winning easily.

We celebrated in Rosie's in front of a roaring fire.

Shorty even did his party piece.

Without warning a couple of pints of seawater gushed out of his nose, right onto his silver fin trophy.

Every year Saltburn celebrates its Victorian heritage staging a "Victorian week."

There are always lots of things to see and do.

It usually ends in a spectacular fireworks display from the pier.

That was until a few years ago when it went low key, due to the lack of funding.

One year during the Victorian celebrations, an iron man event was set up.

Surfers, canoeists and water polo enthusiasts were all expected to show.

On the day of the event 3 of us turned up.

We went through the motions.

A run down the beach, a swim around Nick Markl, (who was acting as a marker in a surf ski), back to the beach and then into a surf ski and paddle like hell around Nick, then back to the beach for a run to the finish.

It all was going so well for me until we started.

By the end of the swim I was knackered; Nick was drifting further out on the ski.

The surf ski seemed a bit dodgy, it kept on tipping over.

By the end I was done in.

Unfit, I finished a distant 3rd.

Luckily I was never going to win.

Tilly picked up the silver rose bowl trophy, from the rather rotund Lady Mayoress.

She planted her freshly painted lips on him, someone shouted for a medic.

The rest of the day was spent sat around drinking, in the car park and on the beach waiting for the fireworks.

Someone suggested a swim in the river, in the large plunge pool.

A couple of lads ran, Parky in front of me stopped.

I carried on and dived.

The pool was usually quite deep, not this time though.

When I came around I was in pain, I had dived into rocks and less than a foot of water.

Blood flowed from my head, arms and legs.

"Fuck, that was stupid", I thought as I sobered up very quickly.

Everyone pissed themselves laughing. No sympathy, no concern, just nonstop piss taking for hours.

I wouldn't expect anything else.

Bastards.

A few more cans eased the pain and I really did see the funny side.

I even asked if anyone wanted to go for a swim again.

An unusual contest was set up by pupils from Huntcliff School as a project.

Surfing in fancy dress.

It was designed for surfers to have fun and express themselves in the water.

A lot of the longboard lads gave it their full support and the local press even turned up.

The entries included a scarecrow, a rugby player, a clown, Zorro, Fred Flintstone, Stevie Wonder, an asian woman, a crashed cyclist and 2 of the ex-presidents, Ronnie and tricky Dickie plus a few others.

After a photo session it was a 30 minute free for all in the water. The drop-in rule was abandoned as up to 6 people shared the same wave, finishing with 2 or 3 on a board.

Nick in the scarecrow costume nearly drowned. He found it quite difficult to do anything with a broom shank through his shirt arms across his back.

Rossy did a bit of a Michael Jackson; he went in the sea black and came out white. No surgery required.

It was an unusual day.

Fancy seeing a president surfing at Saltburn!

EX-PRESIDENTS, rugby players, singers - and Doris - turned up at the East Coast autumn classic long board surf competition at Saltburn over the weekend.

The characters provided the fun part of a serious competition as they surfed in fancy dress.

Surfers from Saltburn and Marske took the honours, with victory going to Gary Rogers (Saltburn), followed by Paul Ross, Nick Noble, Mark Thompson, Mike Smith and John Metcalf.

The next competition will be the

Surfing

Saltburn autumn open long and short board competition over the second weekend in November.

Pictured above in their fancy dress are Alister Lang (Richard Nixon), Evan Tilscher (Ronald Reagan), Mark Thompson (Bovril Clown), Ian Park (Doris), John Metcalf (Fred Flintstone), Simon Palmer (Petal Cyclist), Paul Ross (Stevie Wonder), Jamie Cochrane (Will Carling), Justin Meadows (Edith).

SCARBOROUGH AND CAYTON BAY

Both places are not too far from each other and only a short drive from Saltburn. Both can work from 1 to 15 feet.

Scarborough is a big seaside resort, filled with holiday makers, candy floss, ice-creams, fish and chips, cheap tat shops and amusement arcades as far as the eye can see.

Cayton bay is a tiny place made up of holiday homes and campsites. All very low key.

You're spoilt for choice for surf shops in the area. Vibe, Secret Spot, Fluid concept and Lowbrow all have enough quality gear to supply the whole of England and Scotland.

In all the shops you'll be given loads of help, but beware you will there for ages just having a bit of craic, talking surfing shite.

Cayton bay surf shop has now been taken over by Secret spot. It used to be run by a fearsome woman, who nobody argued with. Not many people bought any gear there, too scared.

Scarborough even has its own Malibu club. More longboarders enjoying the true spirit of surfing.

SCARBOROUGH
SOUTH BAY

A really good beach break. Usually slow and mellow but on occasion it can get fast and hollow.

We used to park the vans on the seafront near the Spa and spend a long weekend surfing and touring the pubs.

It's just a shame everywhere started charging a fortune to park and no overnight parking allowed.

NORTH BAY

Has some really good spots, some rocks and can get gnarly when big.

At high tide the backwash from the coastal wall defenses, can be surfed. It's really weird but great fun. As with South bay, overnight parking used to be allowed but is now frowned upon.

Everyone always enjoyed weekends in and around Scarborough.

A few times, we went mob handed to A the B's Mam and Dad's house, while they were on holiday.

Always leaving the place as we had found it, well almost.

One flat weekend, we went on a massive pub crawl, ending up on the seafront. Between each pub we went to the amusements or on the beach and ate the usual seaside junk food.

Fish and chips, candy floss, ice cream. Someone even braved the freshly caught local cockles and was very sick.

The rest of us either gagged or laughed.

After another couple of pints we started to walk back to the house to get ready for the night.

As we walked past the harbour, I noticed that the tide was well out. Boats rested in the mud.

Two lads ran across the mud flats, sinking deeper and deeper.

Rossy and A the B, full of beer, then had a bit of a mud wrestle.

Crowds of tourists stopped to watch the 2 nut jobs slipping and falling about. They put on a show for a good half hour.

We stayed well back, shouting encouragement.

The entertainment finished with both of them doing "mud angels."

They stank.

They tried to get cleaned up a bit in the sea, no chance.

The smell was a cross between dog shit, rotting seaweed and dead animals. Nothing new there then.

After a few showers and lots of aftershave, we went out on the lash again.

The Cricketers was a good starting place then into the town.

Some went to the casino, most of us managed to get into Scene 1 and 2, a nightclub.

After more beer we stormed the dance floor.

I don't think Scarborough was ready for a mass stomping session.

The dance floor shook, we stomped some more.

The bouncers asked us all to leave.

After a takeaway, we eventually all made it back to the house.

Tash crashed in his sleeping bag on the settee, while we cracked open more cans.

Nicky, A the B's sister, had left loads of cuddly toys all over the house.

One by one they were either put inside Tash's sleeping bag or piled on top of him.

He didn't move, dead to the world.

We even built a pyramid of empty cans on top of him.

Pissed, knackered and bored everyone crashed.

We were all woken by shouting and cans clattering. Tash had turned over, nearly smothered himself with cuddly toys and started to fight them off.

It was like a scene out of Zulu.

Tash coming out the proud victor, a hundred cuddly toys dead.

It was hard not to laugh.

CAYTON BAY

There are 3 main breaks; -

BUNKERS

This is a beach break over a large sandbar; it gives good right and lefts with long rides. A really good consistent wave.

THE PUMPHOUSE

Looking out to sea it's on your far left. Lots of rocks, strong rip at times. I have been caught out here a few times. Still good waves to be had but avoid the rocks as they aren't very forgiving.

THE POINT

I have never surfed it. I have seen it breaking very large and clean on a few occasions. Only for a brave few.

I really enjoy sessions at Cayton but its major drawback is the steep slope back up to the car park. After a long session the last thing you want to do is climb Mount Everest!

I've never been in a competition there but have watched many.

Two of the most memorable, were when Tom beat off some of the top surfers in Britain. "Tiki" Tim Hayland and Howard Davis amongst them. He won rounds in the British cup, longboard division.

Tash entered almost sleeping in for his heat, after you guessed it a heavy drinking session. He did well beating some stiff competition, only to be put out in the semis.

Tom surfed brilliantly through both competitions. It's only a shame that he did not travel to other rounds of the cup and beat the best in their backyard.

There are many pubs and nightclubs in Scarborough some good, some bad. When we made the trip, we'd visit as many as possible. Some we'd get thrown out of. Some wouldn't even let us in but we had such a good laugh in the rest it didn't matter.

The nightlife was always good.

Scarborough and Whitby surfers are all really decent characters (or at least the ones I have met are).

They have the same attitude as myself and my friends. Surf, have fun and party.

It's a bit different now with kids but you get the drift.

Much respect to anyone who surfs in the North Sea on the east coast, whatever your standard.

SOUTH SHIELDS

This is another place that I have never surfed.

I have looked at the beach break on the exposed coastline and always moved up to the breaks in the Tynemouth area.

A group of surfers from South Shields turned up at one of the Saltburn competitions. We had never met them before but by the end of the night they were like long lost friends.

We had a good surf do at Rushpool hall then back to Philmores and as ever a fire on the beach. They invited us up to a competition at their place in 2 weeks time. We couldn't say no.

We checked the forecast, it wasn't too promising but we were going anyway.

We drove a convoy of vans, packed with lager, up and parked in the seafront car park near a pub called "Frankie's."

Everyone was in full no holds barred party mode.

We had a few cans around the vans and went to Frankie's.

We met up with some of the South Shields lads who said that the contest would be cancelled.

We drank more.

Being young and incredibly stupid at the time we started mixing drinks.

The idea of drinking double vodka martinis seemed a good idea at the time, very 007.

No one knew what went into them including the barmaids so we made it up.

6 shots of vodka, 4 shots of dry martini, 2 shots of gin and a slice of lemon.

The first one went down quite well.

A the B said he was going for some fresh air and disappeared.

Ste found him lying on the sand, spew all around.

He got him to his feet, A the B insisted on going back in and drinking more.

After a couple more lagers it was time for another double vodka martini.

The barmaid refused to serve me.

I said "I'll make you a deal; if I can get up, walk to the bar will you serve me."

Yes, was the answer.

In a slightly inebriated state I got up.

Pulled myself together, I walked to the bar and ordered.

As she was making the drink she was shaking her head saying, "this is going to have to be the last one."

No problem.

I sat at the bar with A the B, who was fully recovered.

He was filling his pockets with peanuts, which were sat in front of us.

I finished my drink and said "goodnight."

After a couple of steps I remember falling and then being caught, dragged and dumped in one of the vans.

There were others worse off but I didn't see any of that.

I was woken in the morning by Tom and Shorty trying out and wrecking, Keldy's new skateboard.

I opened the van door and asked if there was any surf.

Anth popped up like a jack in a box and said "no surf but plenty of peanuts" then started to chuck them everywhere.

A good morning would have been better.

For the rest of the day we spent sussing the area out. Desperately looking for a wave.

All in vain.

Back at the vans the drinking started early.

We all made a bit of an effort and got changed for the evening.

Frankie's was our starting point.

The barmaids seemed surprised to see some of us back in the land of the living.

We had a few drinks and wandered down the seafront calling in a few pubs.

Stumbling into one, 15 half cut surfers, saw only a barmaid in the bar.

Where is everybody?

The barmaid pointed to the back room, "private party, women only."

Well we didn't need telling twice, with "no you can't go in there" ringing in our ears.

We bowled in.

I don't know who was surprised more us or the party girls.

Yep, it was a 50th.

The place was mobbed with old women and a few younger ones in their 30s and 40s!

We all got kissed, drinks bought and dragged, literally, onto the dance floor.

We taught them how to stomp; with arms flung in the air stamping on the sprung dance floor we nearly brought the ceiling down.

They taught us the twist. I'm sure I heard a few hips popping out.

All too soon it was time to leave. Some retired back to the vans.

Others went to find a night club to continue the party.

We ended up in a right dive of a place, more lager went down.

We somehow all got split up and then a mass brawl broke out on the dance floor.

I thought, "fuck this I'm out of here", I walked through the middle of the fighting, out the door and kept walking down the road.

A while later in an industrial estate I knew I was totally lost.

Id walked for miles and hadn't a clue where I was.

I turned down a very dark road.

A car with headlights blazing was heading my way. I took a risk and waved it down.

"Could you give me a lift back to my van?" I asked the 5 young lads and lasses in the car.

"Yeah, no problem. Where are you parked?"

I hadn't a Scooby.

I said on the seafront somewhere.

They said that's miles away.

I told them that I'd been walking for ages; then I said, "The vans are parked near Frankie's bar."

Luckily they knew where they were going and soon dropped me off.

Only one van had lights on, I opened the door to be hit by a "fog bank" of smoke. Most of the lads were there squashed into every corner.

"Room for a small one."

We cracked more cans and carried on the party long into the night.

The rest of the lads from the nightclub had jumped straight into a taxi, got a couple of pizzas and returned to the vans.

The bastards had eaten all the pizza.

Next day we drove home. It seemed to take forever.

Tash's van engine blew up.

Not just the puff of blue smoke and the gentle slowdown as you pull into the hard shoulder.

This was a major breakdown. Bits of metal and oil flew everywhere, splattering window screens, as we travelled at high speed.

O.K. maybe not that high, 50ish.

Dod towed him home.

NEWQUAY AND IRELAND

Sat in Rosie's one flat drizzly afternoon. The open fire spitting and crackling.

A few of us, after a few beers, got talking about surf trips and where we would all like to go.

Hawaii, Australia, Fiji, New Zealand, Costa Rica, Morocco, Cape Verde islands (I thought this was a made up place) were all mentioned.

We only had limited funds at the time, so somewhere closer would be more realistic.

The more we drank the more we tried to plan something; Nick recommended Ireland, Gary France.

One or two mentioned Thurso, others the Canaries.

Too many places to choose from.

Was it just another bullshitting session in a pub afternoon or could we actually plan something.

Shorty and Leggy had already planned a trip to Newquay; around the time of the Fosters surf competition which was part of the world tour in late August / September.

We were so impressed, that myself and Tom arranged to meet them down there.

As the trip got closer, Tom suggested that we should try another place as well. Southern Ireland.

I knew next to nothing about Ireland but started to find out more when we booked our ferry tickets.

The great plan was coming together 5 days in Newquay then 2 weeks in Ireland.

Tom's Dads old AA map book to guide our way, Sat. Nav devices were decades away..

Shorty and Leggy were going down to Newquay a week before us, so would hopefully find places to park the vans.

The local council had stopped overnight parking on Fistral beach car park, miserable sods.

Part of the surfing way of life was being taken away by pen pushing money grabbing bastards. As you can tell this gets my back up, every so slightly.

We packed the "splitty" van with all the necessities lager, soup for me, beans for Tom, enough clothes to last, Toms board and his brothers as a spare, (I planned to buy one in Newquay), wetsuits, towels, 2 very large jerry cans for petrol (we'd heard it was expensive in Ireland, so we'd take some with us).

By the time we were ready to go there was little room in the back at all, it didn't matter cos we were going to sleep in the elevating roof bunks, no problem.

Most importantly we made up the compilation tapes which would keep us sane on our travels.

It was a very eclectic mix the Beastie Boys, Big Audio Dynamite, Prince, Run DMC, Housemartins, the obligatory Bob Marley, Chris Rea - on the beach (he lived in Saltburn and travelled on our school bus, before he was famous, nice bloke, brilliant musician). Lots of chart music, which was iffy to say the least. Punk stuff, Mod stuff, some Northern soul and last but not least the Pogues – Rum, Sodomy and the Lash.

We played this cassette to death.

It was the sound track for our adventure.

We sang along to the sickbed of Cuchulainn, I'm a man you don't meet everyday, a pair of brown eyes, Sally Maclennane, Navigator, Dirty old town and waltzing Matilda.

It was just brilliant raucous music.

We said our goodbyes to our families and set off, first stop the petrol station.

We filled the van up and got a free Shell flask. We put in a couple of pints of milk, for coffee and cereal.

The journey down to Newquay was long and tiring.

We arrived early morning at Fistral beach. It was warm, the surf looked brilliant, the water clear blue.

We went surfing.

It was a small powerful day, easy paddle out. Only four others in the line up.

Waves were taken at leisure.

Two hours later, it was like Blackpool.

A million people battling for the same wave, drop ins everywhere.

The once empty beach was a mass of windbreaks and holidaymakers. We beat a retreat.

The search began for Leggy and Shorty, no success.

We trawled the surf shops in search of my new board. I expected loads of choice in the "surf city", but it was hard work trying to find something half descent.

I ended up buying a Roger Cooper dayglow board. It turned out to be an inspired choice.

I put on a full block of "sex wax" and went back down to Fistral.

Battled my way through the sunworshipers, windbreaks, sandcastles, avoided the frisbies, only stopping now and again to admire the view.

I paddled out back, through the masses of surf school students and holiday makers.

As I sat waiting for a wave, I looked around at the others in the line up.

Not too far away a lad with bright white hair took off, he had an unmistakable style.

Leggy.

Further down the line up was Shorty again hair blond white.

"What the fuck have you done to you hair" I shouted.

Laughing he just pointed upwards towards the sun.

"Foooook offf yee daft baaastard" I shouted.

We had a Saltburn reunion on the beach.

The lads telling us tales of the party nights and fighting off the women.

We took everything with a pinch of salt (you know what surfers are like for exaggerating!?)

Back at the vans the lads said "follow us we'll show you where we've been staying", then added whatever you do don't stop, just keep smiling and waving.

We knew they would be up to something, the "chancers."

To be honest we hadn't a clue what they were on about, but as we reached the gated entrance to the Headland hotel we started to suspect.

We slowed up, Shorty waved to the security guard, the gate opened, we drove in smiling.

The guard waved back.

Oh my god, we're in.

We parked up behind the hotel.

"What was all that about?" I asked

They think we're pro surfers, cos the Fosters competition is starting and they are all stopping here.

We changed and went on a tour of the pubs.

The whole of Newquay was jumping.

Sure enough, the lads were approached by lots of women, that they had met over the previous days all seemed very friendly.

What I thought was bullshit, was in fact an understatement of the truth.

We partied all night getting back to the vans early morning, knackered from the journey and surfing I'd got my second wind but now I just wanted sleep.

After less than half an hour, the van door slid open Shorty was saying something about a party on the beach with some girls.

Tom dragged me up c'mon lets go.

We stumbled down the grassy embankment to the beach half asleep, cans of lager and a bottle of whisky in hand.

We were greeted by, the now traditional, fire with plenty of wood nearby, the platinum blondes, (Shorty and Leggy), a large non portable ghetto blaster booming out tunes and loads of mad women.

I was grabbed by two women and convinced to jump the fire with them.

Just clearing the flames, we collapsed in the soft sand, pissing ourselves laughing.

We danced, sang and drank some more.

Some went skinny dipping in the not so warm sea, others disappeared returning in a bit of a sweat...

The dawn rose and we toasted it with a large swig of whiskey.

We stayed warm by the embers of the fire, taking turns to tell stories and just talking shite.

Tiredness had come and gone a long time ago. We all drifted away saying our farewells.

Collapsing in the van, I lay for a while then unconsciousness swept over me.

Hours later I was awoken with a bacon sandwich being shoved in my face, very unexpectedly, Shorty and Leggy had been cooking and it wasn't burnt or anything.

We got up and took in the view over Fistral pure magic. Blue sky and good surf.

We got our towels and tooth brushes, all four of us walked into the hotel past reception.

A young lady smiled but said nothing.

Into the posh toilets we went. We started washing and brushing teeth.

In walked ex World champion, Tom Carroll. (He had won the title 3 times, as well as the Pipeline Masters) he looked at us, a bit taken aback.

"Morning lads", he managed in an Australian twang, before disappearing into trap 2.

It was and probably still is one of Shorty's greatest memories of his hero.

Yep, Tom Carroll taking a dump.

After he'd left, Shorty went into that very same trap emerging with a piece of toilet paper, as if it were the Holy Grail, "Tom Carroll actually used a piece of this toilet paper" he said as if we'd be impressed.

We just took the piss, then got out of there.

The next few days were spent surfing in the crowds, drinking loads and partying hard occasionally bumping into Curren, Ho, Blain and co in the hotel.

On our last night with the lads, we sat in the Sailors kicking back.

I noticed a group of lasses, on an opposite table looking over.

I thought nothing of it.

We were getting lost in surfing tales. I couldn't help but watch as the lasses, on the table opposite, started to toss a coin and point in our general direction.

The lads hadn't yet noticed.

Intrigued, I went to the bar and got the round in.

After putting the drinks down, I wandered over.

The lads shouting what you doing, after me.

"Evening, couldn't help notice you tossing the coin. Is that for who's going to the bar?"

The reply was totally out of left field, "No, were tossing for which one of us gets each of you lot."

They came over and joined us for the rest of the night, more mad women.

They turned out to be working in Newquay, cleaners, chamber maids, etc. it turned out to be another late night / early morning.

The lads wanted us to stay longer but we had to make a move.

We kept in touch through the CB radio, that we'd put in both vans. (No mobile phones then).

We kept shouting come to Ireland but they wouldn't.

So we sang Pogues songs to them.

We lost contact as we drove up the A39 to Bude.

On arrival in Bude, we parked at the back of a large supermarket and headed straight into the town.

What we found was the Radio One roadshow, setting up not far away from the van.

We took up prime positions and set up for the day, surrounded by drink.

It was a hot sunny day, loads of people being well and truly entertained. We even got a mention, Bruno Brookes (Who?) gave us a shout out on the radio. The only person to hear it was Dangerous Jeff.

After it had finished, we pub crawled around the town. It was a lot quieter than Newquay.

In the morning, we drove up through Cornwall and Devon, making our way into Wales and eventually Fishguard.

As soon as we crossed the border it went from brilliant sun, to pissing down with rain.

Welcome to Wales...

We topped the jerry cans up with petrol and stocked up on provisions. More soup, beans and lager.

We arrived at Fishguard, just to see the ferry pulling off the dock, without us.

We had missed it by 5 minutes.

With hours to kill before the next ferry came, the Fishguard Bay Hotel was my idea for something to eat and drink.

At the top of a bank, out of breath, we looked at this impressive hotel.

We walked in, a group of local fishermen talked quite loudly in English about lugworms and other interesting fishing stuff, over in a corner.

I went to the bar and ordered beer and food.

The locals eyed us both up and down, then the ignorant bastards spoke Welsh, obviously talking about us. We picked up the hotel brochure it said something about beautiful views and a friendly hotel atmosphere, we pissed ourselves laughing.

The local lads had a bit of a "hissy fit", we carried on laughing.

We had our food and some drinks and eventually left.

I can still hear the fisher folk cursing us still in English, of course.

It was still pissing down.

The starter motor on the van started playing up, I pushed the van off a couple of times.

Eventually making it onto the ferry.

After a couple of beers, we were now back in holiday mode, after escaping Wales.

In Tom's words "It's a fucking shithole."

From the little we saw of it I had to agree.

We've got a few mates from Wales and they seem to think that we just met the wrong people but as they say, first impressions count.

IRELAND

As were arrived into the Irish port, we went back to the van, with our fingers crossed.

We were parked right at the front and soon realised that we would have to go up a ramp, not much chance of a push start here.

We crossed our fingers, Tom turned the key, the van sprang into life.

We both went ballistic, jumping up and down and shouting.

The coach full of blue rinsers on a Saga holiday, next to us must have thought we were mental.

Off the ferry, the sun came out.

We were stopped by customs, I suppose they didn't get too many red and white 1963 VW split screen vans passing by; especially stuffed with all the gear we had on board.

"Anything to declare" the customs man said.

We replied in unison "Yeah, we fucking hate Wales."

He waved us through a broad grin on his face.

"Have a good trip lads" he shouted after us.

We had decided to drive straight across to the West coast but somehow ended up in the back streets of Wexford.

Miles away from our final destination.

There seemed to be a holy statue at the end of every street, the kids we passed all waved as we chugged by. Lost we consulted the old map book, which was buried in the back of the van.

We drove cross country through Waterford, didn't stop to see the crystal,

Tipparary, yes we sang "It's a long way..." and it was.

Then onto Limerick, where the wind and rain started.

We drove down the banks of the majestic Shannon and onto Listowel.

The window screen wipers were really struggling in the bad weather, we pushed on in the driving rain the Pogues blasting out, as ever.

We ended up in Ballybunnion bay, located on the Shannon estuary.

A favourite holiday spot for thousands of people, but it was out of season and with a force 9 gale blowing the camper van was less than ideal.

We managed to find a sheltered spot overlooking the windswept beach, surf totally blown out.

We didn't dare risk putting the roof up, as we would have gone airborne.

After a long day, there was only one thing for it, we went on the lash (again).

The first pub we came across was a welcome sight, the rain was blowing horizontal, we were both pissed off after a long drive and the shitty weather wasn't helping .

We walked into the pub half soaked.

Four people turned and looked at the strangers, then carried on talking in English.

A young barmaid greeted us, genuinely friendly.

Clair from Galway told us that in the summer the town would be jumping but now it was well and truly dead.

I ordered Harp lager, Tom drank Guinness.

He tried to convince me that we were in Ireland and it was traditional.

I'd tried Guinness once in the Middle house, Marske and it was horrible.

I stuck to the, not brilliant, Harp lager.

After a few more drinks, the now very good looking barmaid left.

We moved on to the next pub in the driving rain. It was even quieter than the first.

I was having major doubts about Ireland.

We toured around four pubs, not many people around.

Clair served us in our last place of call.

A different pub from the first.

She explained that she did split shifts in 3 different places.

Closing time came, with fish and chips in hand we walked back to the van, the wind hadn't let up any, so no chance of putting the roof up.

Tom slept in the back of the van, wedging himself in between all our gear and petrol cans.

I slept across the front seat.

We were rocked and rolled by the wind, every time I woke, I hit my head on the steering wheel.

Very pissed off, I asked Tom if he wanted to swap positions.

For the next night, very quickly he agreed!!

Next day was another nightmare.

No surf, lots of wind and rain. empty pubs.

We again drowned our sorrows.

That night, in the back of the van I was cramped, I couldn't move and I was getting overcome by petrol fumes, fucking great.

In the early morning, both very pissed off, we decided to go to Doolin, a small village further up the coast.

Nick Noble had met a surfer / bus driver called Noel there.

He said that he would point us in the right direction of some good surf spots.

We drove back along the banks of the Shannon, through the street of Limerick onto Ennis and into County Clare.

Hoping that when we reached our destination we could get food somewhere.

Heading for the coast we stopped near Spanish point and watched 40 foot barrelling waves pound the coastline.

As we sat and watched in awe, a sheep dog ambled up and watched with us.

There was no-one else around, we were miles from anywhere.

We later found out, that Spanish point was named after the Spanish Armarda ships and men that were lost during storms, like we were witnessing, in 1588.

The cliffs of Moher were magnificent, dark and forboding, stretching for miles.

In the distance, you could make out the Aran islands (pre-Father Ted) they appeared mystical, as the storm clouds swept in again.

We pushed on along the coast road noting Lisconnor bay and especially Lahinch, it was good surfing territory but today it was very big and very messy.

Eventually we made it to Doolin.

We passed coloured fronted houses dotted along the roadside.

At the top of a hill we passed the magical Doonagore castle which overlooks Doolin itself.

A scattering of houses with one main street.

We drove on to watch waves crashing over Crab island. It was a caldron of white water, large unridable monster surf, not very inviting.

No surfing today.

We parked outside O'Connors pub, next to the river Aille in a bit of a lay-by. It was 10 in the morning, when we walked in.

Through the doors and straight into a shop come post office.
Fruit, veg postcards, bottles, soap etc no-one at the counter.
We walked into the pub where we were greeted by Mrs O'Connor,
"It'll be two pints of Guinness and by the looks of you some food as well."
I hadn't the heart or strength to argue, we waited at the bar.
She shooed us away "go and sit down lads, toasties O.K." then she disappeared.
The pub was dark but cosy, dusty black and white photos of long dead people adorned the walls.
A main dance floor and small booths with red velvet seats.
It was like stepping back in time.
Mrs O'Connor brought out the toasties.
We asked "If it was O.K. to leave the van where it was", she said it was "No problem", then disappeared again, a bit like the shopkeeper in Mr Benn.
After a few more minutes, I went to the bar to see if we could get the drinks, big mistake.
Mrs O'Connor popped up out of nowhere and gave me a lecture on Guinness and sent me packing.
Tom with a face full of toastie pissed himself laughing.

10 mins later the Guinness was delivered to our table by a young waitress, who asked us all about ourselves, what were we doing here? Where we had come from? The usual stuff, and were we here for the festival?

We answered as best we could, I went to pay for the first round and get more only to be ushered away again. Minutes later more Guinness arrived. Magic.

The barmaid told us to pay whenever we left. A bit dubious, I offered money but was told the same thing by another of the young barmaids.

Had we fallen into heaven.

The pub gradually filled with locals and tourists alike, everyone was really friendly.

American tourists coming back to their roots were a good laugh, especially "Betsy" with the biggest tits I'd seen for a long time, who was really OTT.

The drinks just kept on coming, as the day turned into evening, people turned up with various musical instruments and people just sat and played.

God they were good, every single one of them.

Sharon Shannon and her sister, local girls, turned up and blew us all away with some sweet sad songs.

A very old man came up to the musical area.

He slowly moved across the dance floor, his stick steadying his progress, his back bent with age.

He looked like he was a hundred.

A seat was given up for him, half a Guinness put down in front of him and a fiddle handed over.

To be quite honest, I was expecting this very old man to scratch out a tune on the fiddle and then draw his last.

As he slowly picked up the fiddle, I swear something happened right in front of me.

He gave a nod to the other members of the band and took a sip of Guinness.

The old man was rejuvenated, as he ran the bow over the strings he became young again, his knurled fingers became light and danced playing the most wonderful music ever.

He started off with a slowish jig, that got the room bouncing, then followed that up with a full throttle dancing reel, the other musicians going for it as well.

This got everyone up dancing.

After a couple more songs, he finished his ½ and went home.

Everyone stood and applauded as he went.

The dancing continued late into the night. We eventually managed to settle the bill.

I am sure we drank more than we paid for. We left with see you tomorrows ringing in our ears.

We staggered across the road and crashed back in the van roof up for the first time.

We had discovered the true Ireland.

In the morning, I awoke.

No hangover, the sun was out, blue skies, life was good.

We went back into the pub for breakfast.

We were greeted by Mrs O' Connor, "Heard you lads had a good night last night."

She disappeared again, coming back 10 minutes later with toasties and Guinness.

We hadn't asked for it but she was obviously a mind reader.

We sat and discussed what we should do?

We decided to look for some surf, hoping to get lucky.

We travelled down the road to see Crab island again.

There was surf but it was big and messy, huge close outs.

What else could we do but to have another day in the pub...

We were greeted by one of the barmaids "Back already, were you missing us?"

As we sat drinking, a little girl about 3 came in holding a large pink elephant, she was helping her mam gather and clean the ash trays.

She came over to us and said in the sweetest of little girl voice "Pass the fucking astray, will ya."

Guinness was spat over the table, laughing we passed the ash tray.

Her mother came over.

Apologising, telling us that Sinead, picks up lots of words easily.

It turned out that this was Sinead O'Connor (no not that one) was a very straight talking little girl.

Throughout the day, we met more of the extended O'Connor family. All were wonderful people full of stories.

Three of the lasses promised to take us into Lisdoonvarna, that night, to have a look at the matchmaking festival.

The day was spent drinking pints of Guinness, eating home cooked food and meeting lots of people.

We made a bit of an effort to look a little smarter, we had a wash in O'Connors toilets and put on clean clothes.

We even sprayed a bit of deodorant!!!

Again we had a good night in O'Connors, the girls and a couple of their friends all squeezed into a car and we made our way to Lisdoonvarna.

For such a small place people were everywhere. The pubs were packed but everyone wanted to meet us maybe it was the deodorant working.

We ended up in a hotel night club, where we danced and drank til the early hours.

At one point I thought the night was over, the lights came on, the music stopped, the dj said "that's your lot folks."

It was the end of a really good day...then the lasses dragged us into a backroom.

Everyone seemed to be talking gaelic. We got more drinks at the bar and we were slowly introduced around. "This is Jon and Tom, surfers from England."

We shook hands with a lot of people. Everyone in the room ,bar none started talking english. I was touched by how such a small thing can make you feel right at home.

3 in the morning we arrived back at the van, with "See you both tomorrow" ringing in our ears, we collapsed.

Next morning there was a sharp knock on the door.

Tom slid it open, a young Irish bloke stuck his head in and asked if Tom wanted to sell the van.

He made a bit of a face and then stepped back.

An obvious smell had hit him.

Whether it was Tom's feet, the smell of petrol or the result of drinking far too much Guinness, I'll never know.

Tom just said the van wasn't for sale and closed the door.

In search of surf again, the wind had calmed down, so we were a bit more hopeful.

We travelled North on empty roads, we picked up a couple of hitchhikers , lasses from Galway who were on a bit of a walking holiday, (yep your right, lazy cows), hitching on a walking holiday.

We dropped them off near Lisdoonvarna and continued our search for surf.

We came across a long golden beach, which swept on for miles.

There was a glassy swell coming through and no-one else in sight.

This is what we had come for.

Perfect surf, lefts and rights peeling well in the light offshore wind and the added bonus of surfing in the gulf stream.

What amazed me was the cleanliness of the sea, absolutely crystal clear, no sewage, no fear of getting panty liners stuck to you.

This was Fanore beach.

As we surfed, we were joined by a school of bottlenose dolphins.

Around 20 of them, small and sleek.

They just swam in and took over surfing the waves. Swimming back under us we could feel the power from their tails as they went.

It was a privilege to be in the water with them.

They went as quickly as they came but for well over half an hour, we had ringside seats into an ocean spectacular.

We went for something to eat.

Beans for Tom, veg soup for me and a large loaf from O'Connors post office / grocers.

After that Tom went for a walk down the deserted beach, I crashed in the sun recharging my batteries, saving my energy for the next session.

He returned an hour later with what I can only describe as a mermaid.

This lass was a stunner with hair down to her arse and a friendly smile. Tom was obviously in love.

You could tell cos he was drooling.

It turned out that it was the last day of her family holiday (typical), and she was returning to Northern Ireland in the morning.

We all spent a very pleasant afternoon, in the surf or drinking in the van talking shite (we were good at that). We said our goodbyes.

Tom and the mermaid disappeared into the sanddunes. He returned later looking a bit gutted.

They did keep in touch for a while, until her Dad found the letters and that was the end of that.

That evening we returned to Doolin and walked to another pub.

McDermotts turned out to be another gem. It had the best irish stew and quality Guinness.

We finished off the day in O'Connors, which was full.

We were greeted like long lost sons,"Did you enjoy last night", "Good to see you both" and "Have you been surfing today" followed by pints of Guinness, heaven.

This became our daily routine over the next couple of weeks, surf, drink and enjoy the craic.

One morning we made for Lahinch. The van, push started first time, we now had it down to a fine art.

As we arrived it was low to mid tide, the surf looked good but a bit heavy.

As I changed, I soon realised that I was desperate for a shite.

Mentioning this to Tom he said he'd better go as well.

There's nothing worse than been pounded by heavy surf and realise your dying to go.

I've known the odd surfer add to the sewage problem. If you follow my meaning.

Like a couple of penguins half suited up, we made our way to the public toilets.

Tom claimed trap 1, into trap 2 I went.

At this point, I should tell you that I'm not really the squeamish type but as I looked into the pot, whilst lowering my suit ready to put my arse on the seat.

I saw the most disgusting toilet ever in the history of the world.

Not only was there shit splattered all around but crawly little insects scurried around.

I was nearly sick there and then.

What else could I do but offer Tom the swap.

His answer came back quickly and was rather surprising. "yeah no problem I'll swap with you."

I wasn't being a bastard, I was just so desperate.

We shuffled past each other half laughing.

We both did the teeth gritted "foooooking hellllll" thing.

Trap 1 turned out to be worse, more shit everywhere, loads more crawly things.

The gagging reflex kicked in again.

My skin crawled, as I had to do what I came in for.

Tom was just laughing, slightly insanely.

I have never been so glad to get into the water as I was that day.

We made our way down the beach and paddled out.

We had a really good session.

As the tide pushed to high, the waves got bigger but cleaner

I now noticed that the beach was gone, the only apparent way out was to catch a wave jump off and run up the jetty, board under your arm. Easy.

After half an hour and a couple of really calamitous attempts to get out, I decided for a long paddle to my left and head for the distant beach as I set off.

I watched as Tom caught a wave jumping off the wave, slipping and running up the slipway.

He waved "C'mon its a piece of piss" he shouted.

Two fingers told him that I was paddling for the beach.

We both had a fantastic time in Ireland, so good in fact that Tom enquired about a job in the soon to be finished fish restaurant above O'Connors.

He reluctantly decided against it though. I was glad, as I didn't fancy hitchhiking across Ireland with all my gear.

On our last morning, we were down to very little money left, we went into O'Connors to say goodbye to anyone that was there.

We were welcomed in by old Mrs O'Connor, we ordered coffee and a toastie.

We told her that wed ran out of money and that wed just come in to say our farewells.

She made a bit of a fuss and said this was on her, "do you like the Irish whiskey lads?" I can still hear he ask.

Four pints and a few whiskeys later we made our way to the van.

It started first time, no push start the first time for a week.

The whole family came out to wave us off or maybe just make sure that we were really going.

As we drove up the hill passed the castle, we looked back and saw everyone waving.

It was a sad day to be leaving.

We never did meet Nicks Irish friend surfer Noel, the bus driver.

In fact we never saw another surfer at all. They all must have been doing the endless summer thing.

The journey home was quiet as we both reflected on what turned out to be a bit of an epic holiday.

Back in Marske, Tom pulled up on my Mam and Dads drive.

We were greeted by both, my Mam fussing as ever wanting to lend a hand unpacking the van.

She entered for a second, then holding her nose she quickly retreated. "Jesus, that van stinks", we stuck our heads in, looked at each other, nothing. We were immune.

As we emptied all the crap out on the front garden, we came across cans and pans thick with living green mould, the long forgotten flask full of milk was now just pure penicillin.

My Mam was right, it stunk, not only that but we stank, our clothes and bodies.

After a cup of coffee, Tom went home leaving me to have a hot bath and regenerate.

That night we went out with all our friends, recounting good waves and good friends.

A good ending to a great trip.

THE PARTY
31-10-87

Its just a date, a few numbers that mean nothing to most people but little did I know, this would be a life changing date in my life.

Gary, from the surf shop and his wife, Christine, were having a fancy dress party, it being Halloween.
Everyone was invited.
They lived in a large 3 story house, near the railway station, in Darlington 30 miles from Saltburn.

Tom and myself had various relations living there, so we knew "Darlo", quite well.
Every now and then we'd park the vans up in the Model T or Mowden club carpark and have a mad night around the pubs and clubs with the lads. Tash loved the place.

Humpreys, where Gary worked, was a favourite starting place.
We would then pub-crawl around the Green Dragon, Berties, Yates', the Old Dun Cow, the Pennyweight, the Hole in the wall, the Turks head and loads more.
We always finished in a nightclub called the Lucys.
Followed by a pizza, kebab or parmo.

The day before the party, myself and some of the lads, went to the fancy dress shop in Redcar.
There wasn't much selection left and we didn't have a lot of money.
We bought make-up, masks and loads of Halloween stuff.
The party was the talk of the carpark.
Were you getting dressed up? What as? What time are we going?
We had arranged to head to Darlington together in cars and vans, with loads of beer.

I was dressed up as a mad monk full habit, Jesus sandals, wooden cross.
My Mam, the make up artist, helped put scary make-up on, as I hadn't a clue.
Tom and Ste were dressed as zombies, ripped shirts white body paint, bullet holes and blood everywhere, A the B was the devil (no make-up needed there then) leather trousers red and black writing all over his body and Tash came as Dracula.

Keldy was an impressive Frankenstein with 4" platform boots to make his 6 foot something body even bigger. There was a mummy, never found out who this was, a fisherman, a rugby player, Rossy as Ali Baba, fez and all. Leggy made a convincing St Trinians schoolgirl and there were so many others.

We got to the house early and were greeted with Gary dancing. Bottles of Newcastle brown and cans of lager, were handed around.

There were people everywhere, the music was blasting, the place was going off, it was a fantastic start.

People just kept on arriving, the place was jumping.

A couple of the lads hadn't experienced Darlo's nightlife, so some of us decided to go walkabout around the pubs.

It turned out, that we were the only people in fancy dress and every pub was giving free drinks away either shots or cheap bottles of champagne.

The reaction to us was fantastic, lots of women coming up for a bit of a laugh.

Between pubs we were talking to a group of girls.

Kev Elliot soon got hooked up with a "Sue Pollard" lookalike.

By that I mean she was blonde, wore glasses and was a bit dizzy.

Rossy was talking to another girl. She was dressed in white boots, skirt and a designer woolly jumper.

Something clicked between us, as I began having a laugh with Gill.

We shared a bottle of cheap champagne, both agreeing how shit it was.

We sat on a church wall and talked for a bit.

I found out Gill was out celebrating getting a new job and that she was single. Bonus.

The lasses came with us to the next few pubs.

We all decided to try and get into the nightclub before returning to the party.

We joined the queue of people outside "Lucys" nightclub.

We split up with different girls, in case they said no groups of lads.

One by one, the bouncers on the door turned us away.

Keldy was in front of me dressed as Frankenstein, he never stood a chance.

The bouncers just said "No chance Frankie, only humans allowed in here." Which I though for bouncers was quite quick.

Gill got in, no problem.

The bouncers took one look at me and said sorry son.

Gill came back out and dragged me in shouting "He's with me."

As I passed I smiled and pointed at Gill. The bouncers didn't move.

It turned out that the nightclub was packed and I was the only one in fancy dress.

Lasses kept on coming up and asking was I wearing anything under the habit, some making a grab for my essentials.

It was a brilliant, the music was good and we danced in both rooms of the club.

We found a settee in a quiet part of the club, to drink our drinks and get to know each other better.

At the end of the night, Gill wrote her phone number all over me, just to make sure I didn't loose it.

I asked her back to the party but she said that she, had to get back to he Mam and Dads house.

Reluctantly, we got a taxi together and I promised to get in touch the next day.

She dropped me off outside the party house and waved goodbye.

I was gutted that she wouldn't / couldn't come in as I knew everyone would love her.

As I turned around all I could see was total chaos.

People inside and outside going off their heads.

Rat was surfing on a ironing board, it collapsed, Christine wasn't too happy.

I walked into the kitchen there was loads of food laid out, a food fight had happened earlier, the remains could still be seen.

A the B was being put head first into the still hot oven by Tom and Rossy.

Butter smeared all over his head and body, he sizzling and screaming as he went.(A Big Wednesday moment). He only had a few burn marks around his head, shoulders, arms and back but he seemed O.K.

I opened a door, in the darkness I could make out Kev getting to know "Miss Pollard" a little better. Lots of grunting and groaning going on.

In the lounge, the Who were blasting from the hi-fi. Gary and a few others were doing a mad dance in the middle of the room.

Some of the lasses saw me and within seconds I had all my clothes ripped off... believe me that didn't happen very often.

Someone gave me a bottle of Newcastle brown.

Was I going mad?

What the fuck was going on?

What a party!!

A couple of people were asking where I'd been and who's numbers were written all over me?

I explained as best I could.

I managed to borrow some board shorts and went upstairs to see what was happening.

More sex, drugs, rock and roll.

Most of the people I didn't recognise. Some had crashed the party but no-one minded.

Leggy had hitched a ride back to the party from the pubs.

The driver of the car believed he was a schoolgirl and tried to have his wicked way before realising.

I don't think he will wear that costume again. Or maybe he will, who knows.

The party just went on and on. No-one in the house got more than an hours sleep.

Leggy had retired to his van. He decided he was going to be sick, opened the van door and spewed all over the neighbours dog that just happened to be walking by!

In the morning, Lisa woke us all hoovering and full of energy. "Come on, haven't you got homes to go to" she shouted.

Absolutely burnt out we headed home.

Back home and in the shower I tried to wake up a bit.

The phone rang, I ran wet to get it.

Gill and asked if I wanted to go and see the stockcar racing.

I, of course, said yes. I couldn't wait to continue from where we had left off.

She said "See you in 40 mins then."

"O.K." I said and put the phone down.

Fucking hell 40 minutes, I finished the shower got dressed, putting on a clean "Fat Willys" sweat shirt, to make a good impression. (What was I thinking).

Had a very quick cup of coffee and set off on the 30 minute drive back to Darlington.

It wasn't the best ever first date.

Zombiefied was a good word to describe me.

White faced, tired but ready for anything.

Gill later told me that, when I first arrived, she asked her Mam to say she was out.

Luckily she didn't and this was the start of our fantastic relationship.

GILL

Gill comes from Darlington, which lies 30 minutes drive from the coast. A few surfers make the journey to Saltburn but not many.

I thought I was a bit wild until I met her.

Early in our relationship, I introduced Gill to surfing.

On a cold November day, when 6 foot of white water mush was dumping on the beach, Gary hired us a wetsuit and I took her into the not ideal conditions, on my board.

There were a few wipeouts, in which she came up with ice-cream head.

All very funny but I couldn't laugh too much.

She started getting the hang of it.

She paddled out as far as she could, waited for a wave and body surfed it all the way into the beach.

Thankfully, the broad smile told me that she was having a good time and this horrible day hadn't put her off.

She soon had her own Snugg wetsuit and was soon paddling out back, catching and riding "proper" waves.

Gill changed my prospective in the water.

Surfing, apparently, is meant to be an individuals pastime / sport.

Man v the sea, but looking after someone who was just starting out, changed things.

Gill would get a wave and I'd ride the next one in, checking that she was O.K.
I knew that she would be but wanted to make sure.
As she grew more confident in the water, we'd ride waves together.
Sometimes she would get cocky and push me off my board.
Some thanks.
We rode the 11' 3", (see next chapter) tandem at times, that was a real buzz.

We both loved to travel, we saved up and followed our dreams.
We loved everywhere, the Canaries, Bahama's, Jamaica, Cyprus and loads of other places, near and far.
We even found the odd bit of uncrowded surf.

I feel very lucky to have found someone who understands surfing and me.
Yes, I realise it sounds a load of bullshit but that's how it is.

THE 11 FOOT 3 INCH BISMARK

Ever since I had started surfing, it was an ambition of mine to build my own surfboard. Now, I had realised it had to be a longboard.

It was another pipe dream, the type that gets talked about but never get anywhere.
I was talking to Jeff "Riddler" Ridley, one day in Rosies, over a few beers about board building, he agreed to keep me right as long as he could glass some boards in my garage.
Jeff at the time was making some excellent boards under his Planx longboards logo, with some assistance from Big Neil.

He kept mentioning you need to put soul into your board. I hadn't given a lot of thought about putting my surfing soul into a piece of foam but I was about to give it a go.

I was thinking where's Jeff, he doesn't usually leave the car, he usually puts a note through the letter box.
I went back into the garage the heat and smell of the resin nearly knocked me over, I found Jeff slumped against the far wall, very spaced out.
"How's it looking man?" He mumbled as I dragged him out.
Looks fine to me.
He soon came back to normal, telling me that he knew that the resin was affecting him but he had to finish the board.

We sat down over coffee and started talking about my board.

I was planning to make a 9 foot 3" or a 9 foot 7" board, single fin, very much old school.

He phoned Seabase to order the blank resin and cloth.

As he's talking, I realise that there is a problem.

It turned out that there were no blanks of my size in the country, the next shipment due in a months time and that the only blank available was an 11 foot 3".

I was desperate to get started, so I said just get it.

I didn't stop to really picture how big an 11 foot board actually is.

Just so you know, a blank is a lump of foam with a harder outer crust, it has a piece of wood down the middle, a stringer. Some have two or three, a double or triple stringer, this gives the board strength.

Two days later a large van pulled up, a huge huge blank emerged along with tins of resin, cloth and other bits and pieces.

At this point I was just thinking that this was going to be one hell of a board, "The Bismark."

Jeff had left a list of instructions and told me to call, if I got stuck.

Day 1

I carefully laid the blank on the trestles, unwrapped my new power plane and made my first attempt at taking the crust off the board.

Even set at the lowest setting the garage was transformed into a Winters scene in seconds, I couldn't see, I was choking on the foam snow.

I stopped.

In the bottom of the planes box, were bags that could be fitted to reduce the "snow", I found a paper mask and started again.

I reduced the rocker, (the bend in the board), being careful not to over do it.

The outer crust was a yellow white but once that was planed away it revealed a bright white undercrust.

It took a while but that first night I'd come out looking like a snowman. I started to clean up but the foam was everywhere mission impossible.

The board was starting to look something resembling a board, I was quite happy with what it was starting to look like.

Day 2

I had drawn half the shape I was after on some wallpaper to use as a pattern.

After putting in the V of the board, checking everything was symmetrical.

I laid the pattern onto the top of the board, now at this point I was a bit apprehensive, saw in hand I began to cut along the edge of the pattern.

One side complete, I flipped the pattern over.

Before I had realised, instead of cutting straight, the blade had dug in on the underside of the board, cutting an extra ½ inch.

"Shit."

Jeff's words rang in my ears.

"You can take foam out but you can't put it back."

I finished the cut, then decided that my only option was to make both sides match.

Being extra careful I made the cut. No panic.

Standing back I looked at my board, it was looking quite good.

Lots of beer was consumed that night.

Day 3

I started to reduced the boards thickness and plane the deck to how I wanted it.

Snow everywhere again.

Jeff put his head around the garage door, how's it going then "Woooaaahh" he shouted.

He genuinely seemed impressed either that or he was doing a really good impression.

The rest of the afternoon was spent doing the rails.

Rechecking and measuring at every stage.

More sanding and planing.

Day 4-7

These were the hardest days of all. So near but so far to go.

I was getting well and truly pissed off.

More rechecking, planing and shaping.

The sanding took forever. Taking the stringer down again, rechecking everything.

Finally the shaping of the board was finished.

I stood back and actually felt quite proud.

I just hoped that I wouldn't mess things up while glassing.

The garage then got a total clean up, even to the extent of hoovering the floor.

This seems a bit extreme but I didn't want dust spoiling the glassing.

Day 8

The acrylic paints and masking tape came out.

I'd seen an old surfing video with a board with the nose and tail painted in squares of colour.

So wanting a bit of a traditional look, I went for large black and red squares.

I really surprised myself, it looked good.

Day 9-15

With the shaping finished and the garage free of dust, I put the heater on and mixed up the resin.

I'd already cut the cloth a layer of 6oz an another of 3oz.

I laid this on the board and started to pour the resin, the smell was fantastic.

I worked fast with the squidgie (a soft plastic spreader), making sure that the whole of the board was covered, keeping an eye out for air bubbles, working the resin through the glass.

The trick is not to work too long, cover all the glass, get rid of the air bubbles and sit back and leave to dry.

Over the next few days the resin and glass dried.

I repeated the process on the other side.

Before the gloss (a shiny finishing) coat, I put in a fin box and leash plugs.

Smoothed out any lumps and carefully put the final gloss coat on.

I then left the board to go off.

I did keep on going into the garage and everytime was surprised at how good it was looking, it was a work of art but would it work in the water?

Along the journey of building my longboard, I learned what Jeff had meant about putting the soul in there. It was about the blood, sweat and tears, the hours of checking lines and curves.

It was about caring about every stage of the process.

I'd ordered an extra long leash from Many Retuns so I was ready to go, apart from the fact the surf disappeared.

After a 10 day wait a 3ft swell came in.

The board ideally should have been cured for 3 weeks but I just couldn't wait any longer.

The looks and comments I got, in the car park, were brilliant.

There was the odd "What the fuck's that" from the shortboarders, I just smiled and said "That's the Bismark."

My first couple of waves were a bit iffy, then a set came in with a bit of power, the board hit the bottom turn, I hit the back and then just glided.

People scrambled to get out of my way, I just threaded through them. The board was responding even better than I had ever hoped.

My grin just got bigger and bigger.

I paddled way way out back. Waited for a set, paddled and surprised myself by how easy it was to catch the waves very early.

This was what I had been looking for, a longboard that felt right. Something that could pick up waves so early, that it was ridiculous.

Everyone wanted a go on it. Jeff "Riddler" and Tom loved it, Gill thought it was ridiculously big, but still gave it a go.

I just loved cruising and this built my surfing confidence.

Riding a board that you've sweated blood over, takes the whole surfing experience up a level.

I found out what soul surfing was all about.
Riding a longboarding is all about style, spirit and sharing.
The art of walking the board in order to hang five or ten takes some doing.
Especially on a monster like the 11 3."
I tried cross stepping. Time after time. This was going to take a life time.
On the surfing videos the pros made it look so easy.

I had many enjoyable sessions on it and two nightmares.

The first nightmare being at Sandsend beach with Tom and Gary.
It was a storm swell hitting 10 foot at times.
Easy paddle out at the rivermouth, carefully avoiding the uprooted trees that had been dragged down river by the rising water.
As I sat outback I watched Gary then Tom catch some really nice waves.
I broke myself in gently, picking off selected waves, taking the drop bottom turning and kicking out the back again.
Fast take off's, faster ejections off the back of the wave.

The waves got bigger and gnarlier, we shouted to each other that Runswick bay was probably going to be a better cleaner wave.
Tom and Gary caught waves in.
I waited.
I paddled for a monster, pulled out at the last moment or thought I had.
I dropped through the lip of the wave, sucked over the falls, tumbled, hit the bottom, mashed by the power of the wave.

As I hit the surface I could see Gary and Tom in the carpark, they were waving. I waved back, in a help me I'm drowning type of way.

They fucked off to get changed.
Some mates.
My leash had cut into the back end of the board, and partially snapped.
20 feet of parachute string was wrapped around my legs.
I really couldn't move them.
I grabbed the board and body surfed the next wave into the beach.
By the time I had got untangled and got my breath back the lads were changed and ready to go.
As I walked towards them I was greeted by "C'mon we haven't got all day" and "What took you, we thought you were coming out when you we waving...."
My second nightmare happened after I had repaired the board.
I was back in the water after a week and enjoying some brilliant sessions.
One fine day, at Saltburn a powerful 6ft swell was breaking perfectly both sides of the pier.
Perfect lines of swell held up by a strong offshore wind.
Spray flew 20 feet into the air, the waves seemed to break slowly, the faces large and inviting.
It was a perfect day or as close as Saltburn was ever going to get.
About a dozen surfers were in split both sides of the pier so there was plenty of room out back.

After a surprisingly easy paddle out, I sat and watched as a set rolling in.
The first wave I didn't attempt to paddle for, it passed.
The spray from the back of the wave was blinding. Rainbows appeared behind the wave.
This I thought was going to be a good day.
The second wave of the set came.
I paddled, the wind forced me high on the shoulder.
I got to my feet early, I thought I'd miss the ride but felt the power.
I dropped down the face, bottom turned and rode down the line at light speed.
The spray was everywhere, I had trouble seeing, I kicked out.

An hour of this magnificent session went by, I'd had some really good rides.
I felt on top of the world. The tide was pushing up, the waves seemed to have even more power.
I paddled again, now relaxed and in my rhythm, I dropped down the face again.

I heard a loud crack, spray blinded me.
The board went really sensitive then something hit me in the face.
It was more of a slap than a hit, at first it didn't register what was happening.
I was still riding the wave getting slapped, now repeatedly by something.
I grabbed blindly in front of me.
I held what I realised was a large part of my 11 3" deck, still attached...
I kicked out.
I soon realised the board had snapped clean in half...
I paddled in on what was left of the board.
Gutted I scanned the sea for the other half, in desperate hope of a repair.
I knew it was futile.
Lots of people came up and felt the loss.
The mood was made lighter by the onslaught of the piss takers.
Was I now a shortboarder?
Did you leave something in the surf...the rest of your board etc etc

Back at home I assessed the damage. It didn't look good at all.

Later that week I ordered a new blank, cloth and resin from Seabase, this time opting for a shortboard, a 9ft 7".

As a post script, the remaining part of the 11 3" didn't go to waste. It was used for many a repair on other boards, a sort of organ donor type of thing.

119

SURFING LIFE

Myself and my friends had found a lot of the local breaks.

To be honest it wasn't difficult, although the odd hidden wave was found by studying ordinance survey maps or just getting lucky.

We would drive up and down the coast looking for potential new undiscovered breaks.

Sometimes, as we scrambled down cliffs, we got lucky, passing at just the right state of tide.

After we had surfed the secret spot, we would tell the lads in the pub.

We always got the standard answer " Yeah, I surfed there months ago, didn't think it was good enough to tell you about."

Yeah fucking right.

Saltburn

Has 3 main breaks;-

The beach which faces NNE is the most popular with waves breaking both left and right of the pier, depending on the ever shifting sand bars.

It can get crowded but on early mornings you could be there by yourself.

It works from 1 foot to well overhead. Both sides of the pier work well, as does the rivermouth.

Jump off the pier at your own risk.

Penny's hole situated towards Huntcliff, provides fast and powerful waves brilliant when it works. Beware some of the rocks and the strong undercurrent. The odd jet-skier can get in the way as well.

The point, under the shadow of Huntcliff provides Saltburn's most testing wave.

The right hander breaks over hard flat rocks, this provides a very fast barrelling wave.

It can easily be reached via the channel which is the best option when the beach is closing out.

This on it's day can be a brilliant wave.

When it gets really big and heavy, its for only the most experienced. As it will bite you in the arse if you are not too careful.

Nick and Gary moved from the rusty van, to a shop that they had built themselves, next to the pier.

It's like an Aladdin's cave of surf gear, well worth a visit.

Marske and Redcar

Have there own breaks uncrowded, not very popular, but they are what surfing is all about.

Marske has many breaks, the obvious ones are at the Boats, Marske "pipeline", the Graveyard and Stray. There are other spots but local knowledge is key.

The undercurrent can be strong at times.

The sandbars do shift around a bit but good waves can be had.

Redcar breaks include the Groins, Leos, Majuba road and also has reef breaks on the scars.

The "Scars" or reef at Redcar, offer some brilliant surfing but the waves can be fickle.

It's a long paddle there and back and can catch you out.

There has always been a nice break, in front of the recently demolished, Leos pub.

People on Redcar prom, stop with their Pacitto's lemon tops or fish and chips, watching the daft surfers in the cold North sea.

Majuba road is the home to the wind and kite surfing brigade, a hardy lot.
It can be a long and powerful wave.
Respect has to go to Dave and Peter Sands and other Redcar surfers who surfed various breaks at Redcar long before we even contemplated surfing there.

There are always rumours about a new Redcar pier, don't know if it will ever happen.

G-land

Not the Indo classic but one of the pearls of the North East coast.

On its day it is a mawling right hander, big, powerful and mean, not for the feint hearted.

I still class G-land as a "secretish" spot, located right in the heart of industrial Teesside.

There are few, if any, breaks around the world that can be identified by smell alone but G-land is the exception.

It's sulphurous, acidic, chemical and nasty.

Just like the landscape around it.

If your in a really good mood the drive to G-land will start to suck the life from your body, it is a very depressing journey.

Be warned.

I have surfed there many times, you always come out knowing that you've been in a battle.

The rip can be strong, the rocks regularly claim boards and in Winter.

I swear it must be the coldest place on Earth.

When the Winter swells start to arrive, its now become traditional to get a large fire going because everyone knows that your going to need to thaw out after a session.

One memorable day, I and a couple of others chose to spectate by the fire. I wasn't ready to be crushed to death.

A large swell was firing, 15 foot bone crushing waves tore in.

Early on two boards were snapped and their owners battered against the rocks.

Bruised they managed to struggle out.

I saw Tom paddle for the biggest wave of the day, we all yelled from the warmth of the fire "nooooo", as we could see it was going to be a big close out.

I'm not sure if he heard us but with huge a effort he pulled out just in time.

The look on his face was a picture, he knew he'd had a narrow escape.

Tom, Lee, Rossy, Gary, Shorty and a couple of others had rides of their lives, boarding the freight train and hanging on, no fancy moves were made that day. Everyone in survival mode.

Skinningrove / Cattersty beach

Located the other side of Huntcliff, around the corner from Saltburn.

If you want to surf on a desolate beach with few people and fewer surfers then this is the place for you.

Beware the locals, they are believed to eat strangers!

Runswick bay

When everywhere else is big and blown out you are guaranteed a wave here.
The beach and reefs are good.
Its a very picturesque place, picture postcard type.
Its always uncrowded, plenty of room for everyone.
Don't overload the van though as its a very steep bank back out.

S-land

Don't really want to say too much but...S-land is classed as a "secret spot", with a number of world class breaks.

It does get crowded but if you time it right, there are hassle free, waves for everyone.

When it works it takes your breath away. Without doubt, it is one of Britain's best waves.

Take a spare board as many have been snapped here.

Whitby and local bays
Goth central. The birth place of the Dracula story.

Good for fish and chips. In Summer it gets packed out with bikers and daytrippers, parking can be a nightmare.

Amusement arcades and donkey rides on the beach are still popular.

It also has a good friendly surf shop there, Zero Gravity.

Some descent waves to be had but its all about being at the right place at the right time.

Sandsend / Caves

The beach can work from a foot to double overhead, beware of trees coming down the river when there's been a lot of rain.

Caves is more sheltered, some nice smaller waves can be ridden here but you have to catch it at the right state of tide.

For Runswick, S-land and Sandsend also see the wipeouts chapter later in the book.

Hartlepool

Has very ridable waves, have only been over a couple of times to Seaton "canoe" (sorry) Carew and had good sessions.

It can also be a cold, horrible place.

Tynemouth

Has a very good shop the Tynemouth Surf Co. which over looks Longsands beach.

This is a really good place to come and try something different.

There's waves for everyone from the complete novice or when it gets big, to the Pro's.

In Winter it's like anywhere on the North East coast, bloody freezing, but it's always worth the effort.

The local surfers are usually full of good craic. Just don't get them mad cos the tend to start talking faster and sometimes sub-titles would be nice.

There are obviously lots of "secret" spots up and down the coast, all worth getting wet for.

Sometimes its just worth while checking places out, because sooner or later you will find the pot of gold, a bit like a treasure hunt.

"Secrets" the break is obvious but so many people miss it.

"The Cove" unmissable.

A favourite is the well hidden, winter wave "the Bar."

Up until now, I have only surfed it with a few close friends.

I'm sure people will soon be wearing the T-shirt "I've been to the bar."

We all had our favourite breaks but all of us were never far from our surfing home Saltburn.

As the years went by Rossy "the College boy" turned into a cross between a hippy and a Rasta.

He uttered those immortal words "did you know hair is self cleaning?"

Unfortunately no-one told Paul that his wasn't!

He thought dungarees looked really cool.

No-one had the heart to tell him the didn't. Dungarees should be reserved for toddlers or fit young ladies. Not hairy Paul.

Rossy also had a famous security blanket.

He had it for years, it slowly disintegrated, becoming a very poor rag.

Blanket I meant towel, very religious, very holey.

For quite a while Tom sported a jolly green jumper purchased from a charity shop.

I heard that it was, unfortunately, burnt as some sort of surf sacrifice.

We all discovered Vans, comfortable deck shoes. Now World famous footwear. A skate shop in Stockton was the only stockist in the area and he didn't have many pairs. We ended up contacting Vans in Orange County, California and ordering through them. We made up designs varies colours, they were always very helpful.

More and more people were taking up surfing but there was still room at Saltburn for everyone.

We seemed to get a lot of swells coming through on a regular basis but when it went flat madness started to creep in.

We all would check the charts for the slightest of signs of swell.

We sacrificed boards in the faint hope that a swell would come.

Jumping off the pier and having a paddle about, seemed desperate but we all did it.

We drank and smoked various stuff, the lack of waves was pushing people closer to the edge.

We tried skate boarding down Saltburn bank.

The bank is steep, has 2 tight bends as well and a fair amount of traffic going up and down it.

As a confirmed non skateboarder setting off from the top of the bank was nerve racking.

A lot of speed was gained very quickly.

If you could hold on, the first corner could be taken wide.

Keeping low hanging on for more speed into the second corner. Exiting like a canon ball into the car park. easy...it was easy.

Easy to get gravel rash, easy to get run over by a car.

Not so easy to stay on the board or avoid crashing.

I never made it out of the first corner, sometimes falling off within 10 foot of the top.

Battered and well grazed, I left it to the experts.

Tom thought he had mastered it, taking the first corner wide gathering a lot of speed into the second, crouching, leaning out of the second corner.

Rocketing into the carpark.

Nowhere to go but the railings.

As he hit you could hear bones in his hand cracking.

The skateboard looped miles into the air, landing not far from a sand castle making youngster.

After a hospital visit, Tom returned with his hand and lower left arm in plaster.

We were all very sympathetic.

Days later surf came through. He insisted in going in, a plastic bag protecting the plaster cast.

It wasn't the most refined paddle out that I've seen, the annoying thing was that he still caught waves.

One Summers day, after weeks of no surf, about 12 of us set off for a place in the North Yorkshire Moors called Beckhole.

A couple of the lads had found a plunge pool under a waterfall and jumping off it seemed a good idea.

The water fall was only a short walk from the small village, it looked perfect.

The climb up to the top of the 20 foot water fall was a bit tricky, due to the green slippy moss, as I manoeuvred to the middle of the waterfall for my jump to the clear pool below, I took in the scene an idyllic place filled with mad surfers.

I heard a shout " Look out beeeeellllowwwwww."

Leggy crashed through a tree 40 foot above me, arms flailing, he cartwheeled down and belly flopped in the water below.

Seconds later from another ledge Shorty, A the B and Smelly flew by feet first, Tom joined them and then I managed to launch myself into the freezing water.

"You lot are fucking mental." I shouted.

We jumped all afternoon, retiring into a fantastic little country pub in the village.

Leggy hadn't looked comfortable all afternoon. On his first jump he'd been caught in the nuts by a large branch.

Days later he paraded around the carpark showing off his "coconut ball", one badly bruised testicle the size of a large coconut everyone was impressed...O.K., not really that impressed.

In Saltburn, food was essential we dined only at the finest places:-

The Cafe with no name was a favourite and Nicks pizza shop. Parmos and pizzas to give us plenty of carbs to burn.

I have to mention the wonderful lady, Edna, who had the carpark food van.

She alone kept us going on cold winter days.

A big thanks to Heinz for their beans and soup and to the inventor of the Pot noodle.

We started playing 5 a side football, really to keep us out of the pub for a bit.

We entered a Sunday night league, teams queued up to try to kick the "Saltburn Surfers."

What they didn't expect was that we kicked back and weren't too bad at the football either.

The team changed over the years but along with myself, Tash, Wils, Donk, Peter, Dod, Kev, Dan and countless others, we had a damn good laugh.

There were a few casualties and more than a couple of journeys to the A and E department, at the James Cook hospital.

Ste's flat

As I have said previously Ste (Tom and Peters brother) loved the surfing lifestyle, but wasn't to keen on the surfing.

Ste bought himself a huge LT VW van, which on a good day could hold up to 30 people.

He then went one better, buying himself a first floor flat in Saltburn overlooking Marine Parade out to sea.

The flat soon became a magnet for everyone and anyone.

Monty Python videos were played non-stop until everyone knew all the words, Playstation 1 (new technology at the time) entertained many for days.

Parties just seemed to happen.

People would crash for a night or months at a time

Weeks after moving in 2 of the lasses cleaned the flat. They ended up with 20 bin bags full of empty bottles.

It was a serious party house.

Leggy, while sunbathing, outside Ste's kitchen window rescued a parakeet.

They named it Shithead...it had the freedom of the house and was quite friendly, but it couldn't half shit.

During a chilled out night around the flat, something 'strange' happened.

We had done the usual things surfed, then onto Rosie's, the Marine and onto Philmores, ending back at Ste's flat.

The front room was a sea of bodies, on the sofa and chairs, most on the floor.

Music played, the TV was on with the sound turned off.

An unnamed newly acquainted couple disappeared into one of the bedrooms, no-one really noticed.

After 20 minutes, we heard the bedroom door open and through the open lounge door we all saw the lass crawling, naked, into the kitchen.

Not really that surprising apart from the lad she was with was still going for it, making moose noises.

Everyone looked at each other.

The amorous couple then came back out of the kitchen and back into the bedroom still coupled.

The lass was eating a pork pie.

Ste came out with "How the hell did she know that I had a pork pie in the fridge?"

Then after realising, he said "That was my bait for tomorrow, the fucking cow"...

The Wild West Night

The Saltburn surfing community is on the whole a peaceful bunch of friends.

Yes there is the odd argument or disagreement mostly about drop in's.

Disputes are usually sorted without any problems.

One Friday, drinking in the Marine, everything appeared fine.

The place was mobbed, the drinks were flowing and nothing seemed amiss.

There was a shout from the back door, saying one of the lads was outside getting the shit kicked out of him.

Well what else could we do, we piled out.

A large group of lads I didn't recognise were waiting, six were occupied kicking a balled up person on the ground, someone shouted "fucking surfers" then everything went wild.

People were swinging punches, kicks were flying, some really thought they could do kung fu, people were fighting everywhere. It was chaos.

It would have been quite funny watching the "proper fighting", had I not been in the middle.

Lots of swinging and missing.

Kicks miles off target.

Scuffling and lots of holding / wrestling more like come dancing than anything else.

You really did need eyes in the back of your head.

I could see big Neil, a usually quiet lad, dispatch a few people.

Big Dave, a true giant, had one lad on his back trying to strangle him, another at his front kicking him both were sorted out in no time.

In the middle of it all, the other lads were regrouping, more surfers and bikers were still piling out of the pub, (obviously supping up first).

The sound of police cars from every direction stopped things, everyone evaporated.

8 assorted police vehicles turned up, no arrests were made.

They came into the pub and had a look around.

They saw a few people with minor cuts and bruises but that was it, they left.

I'm still not 100% sure what it was all about.

I have been reliably informed, by one of the lads, that trouble was brewing for a few weeks.

Some of the "Rosie's" barmaids were having a small party and their boyfriends weren't impressed when a group of invited surfers turned up and took over.

After the fight night everything quietened off.

Head wetting

It's always been traditional, when a baby is born you "Wet its head" or get pissed.

Over the years, we had a lot of practise, as we turned out to be quite a fertile bunch.

One of the most memorable, (besides James and Laura's, when I can't really remember much), was when Gary and Christine had Evan.

It started in the usual fashion, loads to drink in Rosie's. Topping up in the Marine and Back Alex.

Everyone was having a laugh; people drifted back to vans or made their way home.

Tash, dangerous Jeff and myself assisted Gary back home.
He insisted he was fine but he was buckled.
We got him in and he insisted we had another drink.
He came back with half pints of tequila!!!

After we finished those, Gary filled our glasses again and again.
We all proposed various toasts to the latest edition to the surfing community.
Eventually, he collapsed, we put him to bed.
Jeff said "ring for a taxi."
I really tried but couldn't see the numbers, I was partially blind.
Wicked stuff that tequila.

Next day, I had the hangover from hell and I rarely get hung-over.
The slightest movement and I felt sick. It took all day to recover.
The only good news was that everyone else was suffering as well.
Tequila no more.

The Bug Jam
We were told about a huge event taking place at Santa Pod.
We decided to go.
Everyone loves VW's it's a fact.

The car park was always full of vans and beetles; Some really looked after their vehicles.
Most just abused them.

Through the odd VW purist we heard of a gathering at Santa Pod, the race track, called a Bug Jam.

A weekend with bands, parties and races.

30 of us got organized to go down. We travelled in beetles, vans and a couple of cars.

As we got closer we heard that they were charging a lot of money, per person and not per vehicle, for the weekend.

We managed to conceal 10 people in boots, under beds, even hidden in the roof.

The place was mobbed vans, beetles and other VW's of all shapes, colours and sizes.

We parked in a "wagon train" circle and cracked the first of many many cans. Most people in our camp I recognized but there were a few of faces new to me. There were a couple of strange looking lads wearing make-up...very odd.

One turned out to be Parky.

Someone could easily write a book just on him alone.

He is a true character, a genuine, funny lad, a one man party.

We all, at that time, thought he was bent.

As I've got to know him over the years, I'm still not sure which way he truly swings.

Even though he has a lovely daughter, has been married, has a lovely girlfriend, you never do know.

When they made Parky they broke the mould.

He has fully embraced the surfing spirit and is still a demon longboarder.

Back at the Bug Jam, through the night more and more vehicles arrived.
A plain white van parked near by and was transformed. Everyone taking turns with paint and spray cans.

Before

After

We had a brilliant weekend a nonstop party, drink and drugs everywhere.

We walked miles having a look at all the VW's.

We watched various cars race the ¼ mile as we sat in the sun, lager in hand. The camp fire in the circle of vans was huge; others joined us around it, listening to the blasting music.

No-one actually saw Prousey launch a tin of baked beans in the middle of the fire but when they exploded everyone new.

Rossy and many others got an extra unexpected meal. Tomato sauce was everywhere.

As always seems to happen, Parky tried a similar sort of thing years later, a can of WD40 went into a beach fire.

A 20 foot fireball engulfed Parky. He spent 2 days in the burns unit at James Cook hospital, keeping the nurses entertained.

There were a couple of bands playing one being the Meteors, it turned into a chaotic friendly riot in the area around the band. Ozzie Ste in the middle.

Major hangovers had to be ignored on the long journey North.

Back in Saltburn, we were forming a surf community. A unit of close friends that would encourage and share everything.

We always had a few travelling surfers from Florida, California, South Africa, Australia to name a few.

All were made really welcome and shared in our unique hospitality.

I've heard of localism at various other places around the world but I just can't see the point.

If someone has made the effort to surf the cold North Sea, rather than stay and surf warm breaks then hats off to them.

They'll be welcome here as long as there are waves.

BALI

We had been around Britain surfing and slowly pushed our boundaries, to include other countries.

Now we needed a bigger adventure.

I had seen the films and read the books on Bali, now I wanted the T-shirt.

Myself and Gill, bought the cheapest open plane tickets we could find and set off on our surfing holiday adventure.

We bought cheap as that's all we could afford.

A voyage into the totally unknown.

All didn't go exactly to plan.

The bus from Darlington to London broke down after only half an hour on the motorway, a knackered gear box.

On the replacement bus the air con broke down and we sweated all the way to London.

We dumped our bags in the cheap hotel and went sightseeing Covent garden, Hyde park that sort of thing; Stopping for a drink or two along the way and a Kentucky fried chicken.

Managing to get to Heathrow the next morning o.k.

The flight to Amsterdam wasn't too bad.

We met a steward from South Bank, (an industrial town near Middlesbrough), he was so gay it was unbelievable.

Gay and from South Bank, still for me don't add up, he must have been hard as nails really.

At Amsterdam Schiphol airport, we transferred to a Garuda airlines flight.

It was like a flying hotel.

For some reason they put me and Gill in Club Class, big leather seats, greeted with champagne.

We thought that they had made some sort of mistake but we weren't going to let on.

People around fell asleep or plugged themselves into their laptops.

The stewerdess came around "Hot nuts, Sir."

I pissed myself laughing "Yes please."

It's funny how the smallest things can set you off laughing, usually in the worst places, weddings, funerals etc or is that just me.

After more drinks, we had a quick stop in Zurich and then off to Abu Dabi, where we were allowed off the plane for ¾ hour.

We had a look around the shops, Gill started to look very pale, we shared a can of Cola and got back on the plane.

Gill wasn't looking well at all.

She had a bit of a sweat on but she was cold and very pale.

As we began the take off she pointed for me to pass her a sick bag.

She filled that and another.

Before I could get the stewerdess to pass another, she spewed again all over my Autumn Longboard Classic T-shirt.

I'm sure she never liked it.

We were getting funny looks from other passengers, but it was just one of those things.

The stewerdesses were brilliant they couldn't do enough for us.

Gill fell asleep on the floor, for 8 hours, all the way to Singapore.

I watched the films, listened to the comedy channel and had a few more drinks.

They were free and it would have been rude not to.

As the plane doors opened at Singapore, the heat nearly knocked you over.

Thankfully the rest had brought Gill back to life.

We booked a hotel at the airport information.

A mid priced one, that looked O.K. on the photo.

It turned out to be, as Gill described it "a Shithole."

Small bedroom just big enough to swing a cat, (a kitten in fact), not that we had a cat.

A shower / toilet combo from the 40's or 50's.

Later, we found out that next door there was a Karaoke bar, open until 4 a.m.

Fucking magic.

Jetlagged, we crashed.

We enjoyed our 3 days here though, fantastic food prepared in front of you, woks flaming,

Tiger beer flowing, cheap clothes and electrical stuff, lots of things to see and do.

All the time it was hot and very humid.

3 days was enough.

We packed our gear, it didn't take us long, and rang a hotel in Bali.

I have to tell you that as inexperienced travellers, we only had one hotel number.
We didn't really know what we were doing, sort of making plans last minute.
Hoping that our hotel would be better than the last.
We flew to Jakarta, Java, had enough time to walk around the airport and then off to the Island of the Gods, Bali.
Our pilot informed us that he was starting the descent.
Looking out the window, I could see Bali in the last of the evening light, it seemed quite dark.
It seemed very dark. No lights at all.
My mind was racing do they have electric?
Is ours the only hotel?
I had forgotten to ask how much it was going to cost, shit.
I looked out of the window again, just as the pilot banked very close to the sea, within seconds we had landed.
Runway lights beamed out at us.
"Thank God, they've got electricity."

After eventually getting through customs, we jumped into a bemo taxi (a local minibus), and told him the hotel name.
There was a strong smell in the taxi, perfumed joss sticks smell.
It turned out to be the chain smoking driver. He drove down dark lanes, took a right turn and pulled up in front of a huge stone carved statue.
He pointed. The hotel reception lay just behind.
As we walked in with out bags, people appeared from every corner,
"Take you bags sir", "Welcome", we were given drinks and Gill got a flower.
I'm thinking are we in the right place.
We were shown our bungalow.
We had a bar ,a huge king-sized bed turned back with chocolates, flowers and fruit all around.
A huge bathroom shower and bath.
Outside we were right beside the pool. All this for £20 a night.
"Is the room to your liking sir?"
"Too bloody right," after the last one, this was a palace.

After getting changed, we got a taxi into Kuta.
It's only a small place but its very, very busy.
Cars and motorbikes flying everywhere, people trying to sell you anything you could wish for.
Odd smells entered our nostrils, spicy food from the roadside sellers, with their

little push along mobile cafes or warongs, sweet cigarettes and the occasional smell of raw sewage.

Not much difference from Saltburn really.

As we walked from bar to bar, we noticed tiny baskets on the pavement with flowers and rice in them, offerings to the Gods, we later found out.

Everywhere there were stone carvings of mysterious creatures and gods.

The bars varied from westerised music bars, large screens, big speakers blasting out the latest from MTV to local straw hut bars.

The local beer, Bintang, went down well. Sometimes a little too well.

The first couple of days we went to Kuta beach, we hired boards and had full days surfing, eating, drinking and sunbathing.

To surf in just board shorts in warm water was a pleasure, no 6mm wetsuit needed here.

Yes, we did get hassled to buy things on the beach, but it was all good natured.

We found a pub called the Bounty, not really hard to miss an old galleon in the middle of the street.

We had drinks and something to eat.

Someone put a handful of flyers on our table, one of the flyers said "New bungalows Bali Village hotel £10 per night."

We moved.

The new apartment was only slightly smaller, but seemed a lot friendlier. Offerings everywhere.

We would make this our base for the next 3 weeks.

We hired a motorbike to see some of the sights, the locals don't drive to the left or right its straight down the middle.

Riding through the bigger towns was an experience but once out on the open road it was magic.

I was a bit disappointed at Tanah Lot, it was supposed to be a fantastic temple! It turned out to be nothing really special.

In the books I had read about Bali, this was always one of the main tourist attractions.

Yes, it was a stunning location but it all looked a bit scruffy and didn't feel special. Could have been the long bike ride, don't know.

We got held up on the road people herding ducks, yep ducks hundreds of them heading across the road back to a little village in the hills.

That night we tried the local drink Arak.

We sat at the bar.

Yannie the bar owner, only allowed people one shot, we had ours mixed with honey, followed by quite a few bottles of beer.

It didn't seem to have any effect.

I asked for another Yannie pointed to the sign behind him, "Only one Arak per person, this is good strong stuff."

I explained we were fine.

He gave us another shot each. Followed by more beer.

I felt fine until I tried to stand, my legs gave way, I was completely numb from my chest down with no control.

It was a very odd feeling.

The barman gave us the "told you so" look.

It took ages to get back to the hotel.

We crashed out. No more Arak for us.

Back on the bike the next day, we visited the temple at Ulluwatu, this was what I had expected. A ruin but you could feel it was a special place.

We put on sarongs, as you have to, and walked around the remains of the temple.

The view was breathtaking, sheer cliffs and lines of surf below us.

Hundreds of monkeys strutted, ran and played. Most were friendly but the odd rogue nipped and bit you.

On the way out of the temple, we spotted some "road works" going on.

A gang of 6 women were repairing potholes in the road.

It was a very hot day and some of the women were walking about with boiling tar, in buckets, on their heads.

That's Bali for you...

We rode the bike down a rocky, rubble 2 km track down to Ulluwatu beach.

We parked the bike and walked down the steep steps.

At the end of the track there was, what I can only describe as, a magical sea cave.

Sea and beach one side, us the other.

We climbed down the bamboo ladder very gingerly. It didn't look too safe.

Gill let me go first, cheers.

Once in the cave knee high in seawater, we had to time our run to the beach, as the waves were pushing hard into the cave, 1-2-3 run.

We came out on Ulluwatu beach a small strip of sand, with 10ft barrelling waves grinding in before us.

Only ten people on the beach and a cluster of locals ready to sell us something.

The waves looked brilliant. There seemed to be a couple of perfect peaks breaking over the reef, creating long barrelling waves.

Six surfers were in. I watched in awe.

I was a bit frustrated that I didn't have a board with me but was glad just to be there.

At first, I thought that this was too far a step for me but as I watched I became convinced that I could hold my own...maybe.

Two local women came and tried to sell us everything, massages, T shirts, ice-cold drinks, you name it they could get it.

We spent the full day sunbathing and bartering on and off with the two women, drinking and eating with them in a paradise place.

At the end of the day, we ran through the cave and up the bamboo ladder.

It was only then that I noticed a couple of bamboo built shops above us on the hillside hidden away.

We walked up and checked them out.

One was a place where you could get food and sit outside with a drink, not a cafe or a restaurant more like someone's house.

Next door was a small surf shop, it had everything that you could wish for.
I told the owner that we'd be back. He smiled and bowed his head not really knowing what I was saying.

That night we toured the pubs, in the Sari club (the one that was blown up years later), we met some lasses who were travel agents over from New Zealand and a couple of lads from Oz.
We drank all sorts of concoctions and then the Ozzies taught me how to chug cans of Victoria bitter.
A small hole was cut in the can and at the right moment the ring pull pulled.
This sent the lager out of the hole at a fair rate of knots and if you didn't swallow straight away it went everywhere.
Filled your mouth, went up and out your nose, good for a laugh. It was a fantastic night.
We all staggered to a nightclub and partied until early morning.

Next day, both of us had the hangovers from hell.
Bali belly kicked in and we took it in turns to use the toilet, (very civilised).
I personally could have easily shit through the eye of a needle.
You get the picture.
I'm sure everyone has been there, sweating and shivering, short of breath, wanting to curl up and die. Sipping water, feeling worse. The room not only spins but the walls start closing in and moving out.
Major league stuff.
Eventually in the late afternoon, we made it to the side of the pool, laid down and slowly came round.

At 4 o'clock, a waiter came around with tea and cakes for everyone.
The local chemist sold us some pink medicine.
We took it and returned to the pool.
Still feeling fragile, I ordered two beers, (Bintang), kill or cure.
The toilet wasn't too far away, within running distance.
We both drank the beer slowly.
No side effects.
I could see the colour coming back into Gill's face, with a bit of caution we ordered another.
That night we walked down Kuta / Llegian beach watched the sunset and chilled out.
We spent the next day on the beach, hired surfboards and rode clean 6 foot waves.

I was loving it, not just for the surfing in board shorts in warm water thing but for experiencing Bali, it is truly a magical place.

I got inside small crystal clear barrelling waves, by luck rather than good judgement.

The times I made it out, I was shouting out with pleasure.

It was like watching a video, the pros do it all the time and make it look effortless.

I got lucky, I seemed to be in the right place, the wave helping me.

It doesn't happen very often.

The smile on my face was soon wiped off, as I was sucked over the falls and mangled in a torrent of water.

It was so good to be in the water.

We decided to be tourists and booked an island trip.

At the crack of dawn, yes 8a.m., we got on the minibus to go to Batubulam village for the traditional barong dance.

It was brilliantly done dancers and paper puppet and a lot of "bingley bongly" music as Gill called it.

We went to Celuk to see all the people selling silver and gold, and to Mas for the wood carving.

We went to the volcano mount Batur where more people tried to sell us things by the roadside.

Next to Bedulu and the elephant cave not really much there, same people trying to sell us stuff. Were they following us?

Next the artist village of Ubud, now this place was really laid back, you could walk around and no-one hassled you.

The art was brilliant from traditional to modern.

Got back to the hotel absolutely knackered, showered had a meal in the hotel and went out.

Everywhere we went the bingley bongly music started, on and on and on.

You had to laugh, it would have driven you insane otherwise.

After a couple of days just lazing about, we decided to hire a car for a few day and go and explore the island.

We hired a Suzuki jeep and headed off towards Candi Dasa.

The map we had was to be honest a bit vague.

So it wasn't long before we got lost, didn't panic, eventually ended up going through the Monkey Forrest at Sangah. Then headed for Lovina beach as this didn't seem too far away on the map.

We drove and drove through the mountains the roads turning into bumpy single tracks.

We were lost.

We were looking for a volcano and crater of Kintamani to get our bearings.

Asked some local kids directions but they couldn't understand me.

"Is this the way to Kintamani" I asked.

They all smiled.

"Kin-ta-man-ee" I tried a bit slower.

They laughed.

I did my best volcano impression then pointed to the map.

One of the smiling kids shouted "Kintamani, Kintamani" and pointed further down a disused track.

We all waved and smiled like lunatics at last we were on our way.

The track got worse, now and again I got out to move huge rocks.

The road twisted and turned, after about an hour we reached a pot holed tarmac road at the top of a hill.

We looked back to where the smiling helpful kids had been.

Very close to where we had been the tarmac road went.

We'd been stitched up.

Instead of a two minute journey it had taken an hour.

The little bastards.

We continued our version of the Paris Dakar rally, views were breath taking but we just wanted to get there, after more pot holed roads we arrived.

Sighs of relief all round.

We stopped at the Celuk Agung cottages, really smart place but not many people around.

We had a few beers, swam in the pool and chilled out.

We walked down the black sand beach to watch the sunset and check out the surf.

It was a truly beautiful sunset, no surf though. If you could freeze that moment in time, it all seemed very romantic.

As we walked back to the local bars through the paddy fields, in the semi darkness, millions of bats came out all shapes and sizes, just missing your head.

It was like something out of a horror film.

The fruit bats were huge.

It got a bit unnerving, we hurried to the bars.

It turned out to be a quiet night, we were in a ghost town. The night was hot, no air con, just a fan that made it even hotter.

Somehow we survived.

The next couple of days, we found our way to Candi Dasa no missed turns just straight there.

Booked into wait for it the Candi Dasa bungalows, really smart place again.

We had fantastic sea views, air con even a telly.

Offerings, flowers, statues and small temples everywhere.

Got talking to the barman about the surf; "you should have been here last week, it was thiiis big."

Yeah right, cheers mate but now its flat.

We had a Vietnameese meal, in a cusion filled bar/ restaurant, very cool.

I'm sure bat was on the menu.

We moved again to Sanur, didn't think much of it so moved to Nusa Dua.

This could have been anywhere in the world a large group of hotels filled with posh fat rich people, I suppose that they have to go on holiday as well.

I know we were tourists but at least we were trying to see a bit of the real Bali.

Went to Tangun Benoa got hassled a lot for watersports. This pissed us both off a bit.

We talked over a drink and decided that our favourite place was back at the Bali Village hotel.

When we got there, we were welcomed with drinks and flowers and a basket of fruit.

We'd only been gone a few days!

The next couple of days we visited loads of places.

Padang Padang was a favourite not much there a beautiful beach, one cane shack selling drinks and jaffles (toasties).

The surf was good but I new that Ulluwatu around the corner would be better.

We parked up at the top of Ulluwatu and walked down the bumpy track eventually reaching the shacks on the side of the hill.

We had something to eat and watched the 6-8 foot sets coming in.

We made the quick run through the cave.

I hired a board, set Gill off sunbathing on the beach and started to paddle through the shore break.

Over the top of every wave the next paddle I kept touching the reef, I was starting to have a couple of doubts about this.

Out back it was quite hard to maintain your position the rip was strong and dragged you to the right.

The water was so warm and clear.

My first wave at Ullu was unforgettable, I watched a mellow set roll in, I paddled, took the drop and cut back.

This mellow wave was turning into a freight train.

I looked back for a split second, a huge blue green barrel was closing in, I can't remember if I kept my nerve or just froze.

The barrel came over my shoulder, I felt like I was being sucked backwards.

Noise was starting to get blocked out, I ducked slightly and touched the inside of the wave.

I was buzzing.

I saw the lip of the wave overtake me, the lights started to go out I was completely covered.

For milli seconds, it was a fantastic feeling and then it went dark, the wave closed out...

I remember trying to shout "Shiiiitttte", too late.

I was tumbled onto the reef, sucked up and slammed on the reef again, the washing machine ride lasted for ages.

On the surface I grabbed a few breathes and paddled out back again.

I was joined by and American in a Gath helmet.

"Nice wipe out man, you should have one of these, (tapping his helmet)."

Soon he was off ripping the place to bits, strong slashing cutbacks, ariels, the lot.

Never did find out his name but suspect he had a lot more surfing experience than myself.

Had a couple of O.K. rides, and more wipe outs, the rip made paddling hard work.

I caught one last wave, managing to surf right into the cave.

What a place.

Battered bruised and knackered, I saw Gill on the beach haggling for T-shirts.

I dripped over her, "Did you see me out there?"

"Not really, I only got a couple of photo's. I couldn't tell which one was you."

"Why don't you go back in again..."

I had surfed Ullu and got some minimal reef rash but I was so stoked, even though Gill had missed most of it.

The rest of our adventure was spent surfing Kuta / Legian and touring around finding unnamed breaks, some really good, some average, all uncrowded.

We did a lot of shopping and partying.

The beach parties on a night were a good laugh.

The aim get fed, get drunk, have a laugh and meet lots of new friends.

Everyone we met had a story.

During our days on the beach we got plagued by a lot of people trying to sell you stuff.

Many used the straight fuck off or just ignored them.

We actually got to know a couple of them quite well.

Ketut was our favourite he could get you anything, drinks. Food, paintings, carvings, T-shirts, sarongs, etc, etc. He loved to haggle.

His dream was to buy a brand new 125cc motorbike, he carried a picture of it in his wallet.

Ketut kept all the unwanted hawkers away from us.

We talked for hours about Bali and our world.

He hadn't a clue where we came from so we drew maps in the sand.

We got his life story, he told us how he lived in the mountains with his wife and kids.

He told us that there were only four male names in Bali.

The first son was always called Wayan, then Made next Nyomen then Ketut. If they have five sons then they just start again.

All the families were large 12 plus, obviously they didn't have a TV.

On our last day, we gave him our beach bag that had taken a shine to and left some money in the pocket.

He presented us with a carving that we still have today.
Leaving Bali was really difficult as we had grown to love the mixed up place. From the chaos of Kuta to the quiet places.

The journey home was a nightmare, delays made bearable by lots of beer and good company.

All to soon our Bali adventure was just a distant memory but "the Island of the Gods" still holds a special place in our hearts.

Jon Metcalfe

THE VAN

I was in need of a van.

Not to fit in, just for practical reasons.

Freezing your tits off in the middle of Winter in a hale storm wasn't much fun.

When I first started surfing my car was a white Chevette hatchback, a horrible piece of junk but it did its job getting me from a to b.

It was a cheap car, cheap to buy, not too bad to run and a bonus was, that my surfboard fit in with the passenger seat wound back.

The back seats folded down, so sleeping in it wasn't too bad.

The more I saw the vans down the carpark the more I fell in love with them.

The classic VWs, splitties, wraprounds and the very occasional samba vans with loads of windows.

Tom bought Jeff's red and white splitty, Shorty and Dod got type 2s.

Leggy got a horrible little Fiat van (the pie mobile).

Keldy got a white type 2.5 van, we all got really high the weekend he stuck carpet on the walls and roof, extra insulation he said. No drugs just the glue fumes.

Everywhere you looked in the carpark there was a van of some description, in all sorts of states.

And what did I get... a Ford Escort laser.

Another bag of shite, can't remember why I got it...

Anth got a purple type 2.5 and crashed it on his way to Scarborough.

Tash traded in his XR3i for a type 2 and painted it purple and yellow, he said he got the paint cheap. No-one believed him.

The trips away were brilliant, but I was always in someone elses van or in my car.

Myself and Gill had been down to Newquay a couple of times using here Mam and Dad's 30 or 40 year old tent, it was brilliant but a van was what we really needed.

One day just as the Escort engine and gear box were blowing up, I sold it.

Car less I got the local Exchange and Mart, I went straight to the camper van page.

There I saw a VW, a red type 2.5 Devon van with elevating roof fully equipped cooker, fridge, sink etc

4 berth looked back at me...£2000.

With a bit of help I scraped the money together and with Gill went to see it in Catterick Garrison, an army base, 40 miles away.

A youngish couple had it, climbing enthusiasts, they were getting posted abroad so had to reluctantly sell the van.

As soon as I went on the test drive I knew this was a special vehicle.

The couple lovingly showed us everything about the van the good and bad points.

It was just what we'd been looking for.

We bartered a little and agreed a price.

I sorted the insurance, signed the documents and that was it, we were off.

It wasn't fast, 70 tops, but the driving position was so high it was like viewing the road from the top of a cliff.

The steering wheel was big, no huge, bigger than a bus.

The noise of the air cooled engine chugging along was music to my ears.

The faint smell of petrol.

Gill followed behind in her car.,

Cars passed me on the motorway, kids in the back seat turned to look.

Some even waved, in the age of total ignorance and lack of communication the van put smiles on peoples faces. Why I don't know, but it did.

I continued homewards, enjoying the experience of my own van.

The sun was out, not a cloud in the sky and that smell of petrol.

Oh shit that smell of petrol was stronger, just over half way home I decided to stop and investigate.

Gill pulled up behind in the layby.

"Whats up?"

"Don't know just keep on getting the smell of petrol from the back."

We lifted the back shelf cushion out, then I figured out how to get the engine cover off.

I looked and saw a bloody big engine and some other stuff.

I noticed a pipe was cracked and had petrol dripping to what I later found out was the petrol pump.

I wrapped some tape around it and decided to try to get home.

After all I was insured 3rd party, **fire** and theft.

It wasn't a particularly long journey but I've never looked in my rear view mirror so many times. Expecting flames to start at any time.

Gill didn't really help matters flashing her lights, pointing then pissing herself laughing.

Gill helped me to tidy the van up.

She made new curtains and a matching duvet cover.

Now we were ready for anything.

Our first couple of trips were to Scarborough and Cayton bay, both really good surf spots and fairly close to home.

On one trip, the accelerator cable snapped while driving near the Runswick bay turn off, on our way to Scarborough.

Luckily, the couple who sold us the van gave us a lot of spares and we found a new cable in one of the cupboards.

It was fitted roadside, after a lot of swearing, we carried on our way.

It was a hot summer so we took our 3 year old niece, Joanna, along with us to experience the surfing lifestyle.

Our daily routine was simple breakfast, surf, paddle and build sandcastles, sunbathe, have a picnic, more time in the water and on the beach.

The odd shopping trip and the obligatory donkey rides.

Joanna would disappear under 2 duvets in the van and fall asleep.

When we'd find her she was soaked in sweat and in need of lemon top ice creams and slushes.

The clutch gave up on one of our local trips to Cayton, we were very unceremoniously towed home.

After it was fixed we decided to brave a longer trip, we spent time in Woolacombe, Croyde, Saunton we surfed and chilled out.

Van life was simple. Gill got her own board and loved surfing, not so much the wipeouts though.

We moved down to Perrenporth, surfing really mellow waves, small and breaking perfectly and surprisingly not too crowded.

St Ives was good to look around but the hills were a killer.

We ended up stopping at Sennen cove near lands end. There wasn't a lot there but the surf was good.

We did the tourist thing and went to Lands End.

It was very disappointing and served the worst lager ever.

Warm, flat and cost a fortune.

On our way home we had a couple of days in Newquay and had a really good time.

5 miles out of Newquay on the way home, we hit a traffic jam, we moved a couple of hundred yards in 2 ½ hours.

While other motorists looked on, Gill opened the sliding door and cooked a meal.

I put the table up, set it and opened cans of lager.

All around us was chaos, we just chilled out.
That was possibly the best traffic jam ever.

Over the years we had many trips away in the van, mostly in search of surf.
One epic journey, took us from the North East down to the South East coast and over to the South West, we found a lot of good uncrowded spots but some really horrible places.
We were battered by high winds in Brighton and nearly flooded out in Brixham.
Finally, finding good surf and sunny weather in Dorset, Devon and Cornwall.

When it was flat, we had trips to the Lake District.

The van wasn't too good on the steep passes but somehow we made it.
We'd end up in the middle of nowhere with only a pub nearby...

In winter the van really came into its own.

In the morning if there was surf. The cooker would go on to warm the van up, I'd get changed, leaving the cooker on one gas ring turned low.

I'd surf for a few hours in the hail, snow and occasional blizzard. Then jump back into the warm van.

Pure bloody ecstasy.

While others were outside getting changed by their cars in the cold.

I could take my time changing.

Wiping the condensation off the windows, watching very cold people hop about trying desperately to keep hypothermia away.

I had plenty of people knocking on the door saying "Let us in, its fooking freezing out here."

The kettle always went on.

At a friends wedding, the van was decorated with ribbons and balloons, not really a conventional wedding car.

Over the years little problems turned into major headaches.

The petrol gauge never worked.
Dave Prouse gave me a welcomed lift, to the petrol station on more than one occasion.

The exhaust was constantly blowing,
The twin exhausts were forever being patched up. Catty, baked bean cans and lots of welding.

The heat exchangers packed up.
Not a problem in the summer but in the winter it was freezing without any heaters.
There were days when I had to scrape thick ice from the inside of the windows.
The only way around the problem was to put the gas cooker on low, I'm not sure if that was strictly legal as I was driving along, my legs wrapped in a sleeping bag.

One fine day, I decided to take the exhaust and heat exchangers off to see if I could botch them up properly.
Gill was getting sick of the booming exhaust.

I had a pit in the garage so I thought it would be no problem.

As I took the last bolt out, I suddenly realised the whole set up was heavier than I had thought.

With both hands well and truly pinned under the exhaust, there was only one thing to do.

I shouted Gill.

Nothing.

I tried again.

Ten minutes later she wandered into the garage,

Do you want coffee?

No, I want you to get this fucking exhaust off my fucking arms...

She guessed that I wasn't too happy.

Between us we freed my hands and arms but I was stuck in the pit with nowhere to go.

After a couple of phone calls the lads turned up, eventually dragging the exhaust and me out.

Premier league piss taking took place, over cans of lager.

Days later, it took four of us to get the patched up exhaust back onto the van.

Rust.

The curse of many a camper van. It started to get a grip. It was a constant battle to keep on top of it.

Lots of other little things started to go wrong, all the time...We both loved the van but I'd had enough.

I sold the van.

SURFERS AGAINST SEWAGE

When I first started surfing at Saltburn, it was obvious that there was a sewage problem.

For most of the year, the raw untreated sewage was pouring straight into the sea, right into my new playground.

It had passed through a couple of large grid type filters, to break the lumps up and take out the larger bits of waste.

Untreated sewage, condoms and various female products made the sea around Saltburn, a breading ground for bacteria.

All of the surfers, at one time or another, came down with coughs, ear ache, sore throats and one caught a type of hepatitis which sent him yellow (jaundice), he was quite ill but we couldn't resist taking the piss.

A brown slick could be regularly seen coming from the out flow pipes, but the waves were good and a little bit of shite wasn't going to stop us.

We had to laugh, when coming to the surface from a wipe out you'd find one of those sticky female pads stuck to your board or worse wetsuit.

One surfer had a wipe out at the point. He came up with a string on his face.

I can still hear him say "I hope its a tea- bag."

Seconds later "Nooooooo" as he realises it was a tampax.

Years later, I found out Billy Connelly had done a joke very similar to this piece of reality.

I wonder if he was in the water with us?

Something really needed to be done.

Nick Noble, a strong environmentalist, and a few other local people, made us aware that we could actually help.

In the early 1990's surfers against sewage (SAS) was born.

It all started in Cornwall but quickly moved country wide.

Nick and others organised events / protests to highlight the problem.

The press loved it, pictures of surfers wearing gas masks appeared in nearly every paper.

My personal favourite was a 20 foot inflatable turd, that really grabbed people's attention.

SAS also provided the solution to the problem;
Full treatment of sewage, so that only treated water is discharged into the sea.
Making it not only cleaner but a safer place.
The water authorities must have been spewing when the government started to take notice.
A guaranteed vote grabber.

European legislation is now in place which determines water quality in U.K. rivers and beaches.
Vast improvements have been made but standards have to be maintained and further improved.
Check out the SAS website.

Around 1995, after lots of campaigning against Northumbrian Water, things started to happen around Marske and Saltburn.
Millions of pounds were spent on a treatment works and large storm tanks.
The water off the Saltburn / Marske coastline visibly changed.
Things aren't perfect but have definitely improved.

Surfers' sea sewage protest

Evening Gazette

Thursday, July 23, 1998   Serving Teesside for 125 years   Late Final

■ £20m clean-up boost for our coastline

Turning the tide

Story By

Digest

**icket club
ys price**

GM Cricket Club has had
SB Premier league division
out after fielding an
for San Lorton player under
rookie.

...top of decision was
els held to sell one for
seed. It has been banned
senior chip competitions for
two. Skipper Roy Myers has
been handed a ban.

■ Full Story: Back Page

ts of lolly

...were waterpof last night's
al Lottery jackpot of
,147. Winning numbers: 26,
47, 35, 34. Bonus 23.

oad to safety
—see Page 13

Lers to Right on P2

Tuesday, June 9 1998   **Local news**

Picture by
TERRY REED

Surfers dash to protest over sewage

■ CLEAR MESSAGE:
Banners calling for better
sewage treatment welcome
fed-up surfers - some in gas
masks - who race into the
sea at Saltburn in a protest.

Story by DAVE ROBSON
SURFERS and other
water users went for a
dip in the briny to make
their anti-sewage protest.
Wetsuit-clad protestors -
some wearing gas masks -
braved the chilly North Sea to
get their message across.

Banners were also being
flown from Saltburn's historic pier
in a protest against
Northumbrian Water's sewage
treatment policy.

Campaigners claim people's

health is at risk.
Nick Noble, of Surfers
Against Sewage, said: "The
campaign is paramount to the
organised treatment
improvement should be
as far as implementing
primary treatment.

"We, and other
environmental groups, say
this is not good enough and
that full treatment with
disinfection should be
implemented."

From MP David Bowe
Labour's environment

spokesman in the European
Parliament - backed
Sunday's protest.

Northumbrian Water say
they are waiting for the
Government to make a
decision on the level of
treatment.

As a post script to this, I have to apologise to Kev Ward, for accidentally putting my longboard in front of his face just as the Evening Gazette photographer clicked the shutter.

On the photo above from the Teesside Times you can just make his head out.

This was at a SAS protest organised by Nick at Saltburn, the photographer wanted us to line up and run into the sea and do a bit of surfing, which we did.

Kev had always wanted to be in the Gazette, to show his Mam, but somehow my board fell in front of his face. At least his legs made it...

MORE SURFING LIFE

After years of surfing with very few women, things slowly started to change.

The womens surfing community swelled from being Lisa, Christine and a few others up to at least a dozen hardy ladies.

Lasses who embraced the surfing spirit (and some male surfers), wholeheartedly.

Youngsters started to shine Ledge, Gerry Lopez, Robbie "the pro", Levi, Chris Erie, Jake, Doc, the Andy's Cummins and Mawson, Bart, Jamie, the slightly older Jason "the ginger prince", Diamon Dave, Big "D", Jed, ever smiling Comcast Richie, Tom's old next door neighbour, and so many more.

Levi got a brand new Free Spirit board, first time out, he wrapped it around the pier. Tragic.

Ledge, even when he was 13 was a talented surfer. Obviously we didn't let on.

He wanted the whole "surfer" experience.

One night he was smuggled, under a coat, into Philmores during the rave scene.

For 15 minutes, he took it all in until the bouncers spotted him and sent him packing.

The story goes, a careers teacher, days later, asked him what he wanted to be?

Ledge answered truthfully, "an International surfer and DJ."

"Of course you do son, of course you do!"

When a little kid called Mike Smith turned up, everyone took one look at this blonde haired lad and he was instantly christened "Bart."
He turned out to be bloody good on a longboard as well.

They all changed from annoying squeaky kids into very accomplised surfers.
Travelling much more than we ever did.
They did have a little respect for the older surfers, allowing us the odd wave.

While we were surfing, van security was never a problem, as soon as we put wetsuit were put on for the start of a session, a plague of grommets would descend. All doors and windows were opened, music would be turned up full blast.
Headlights would be flashed in time with the beat.
Food, lager would be consumed. Dope smoked.
Hats, sunglasses, clothes would be tried on. Surf and porn magazines would be pulled to bits, the best pictures stuck all around. The van would be turned upside down but it was safe.

Rossy turned up one day, having had a scorpion tattooed on his leg.
"It's got a sting in the tail you know", we looked at each other then pissed ourselves laughing.
Rossy was flooded with questions, did it hurt?, why a scorpion? Why on your thigh? Why?
It must have made some impact, because loads of people started to get various good and not so good tattoos.

173

Ozzie Ste was the first lad I'd seen with his nipple pierced, that didn't really appeal.

One Friday night, sat at the magnet table, in the Queens. Donkey Al announced that he'd "Had a Prince Albert piercing."
I hadn't a clue what he was on about.
Donk, had had it done the previous week and told us that it was fantastic and that his sex life was "Out of the fucking world, mind-blowing."
Ste started to say "Nah you haven't had that done",
Donk stood up, dropped his trousers and lobbed his cock on the table.
The pub was quite busy at the time, loads of people stopped and stared.
Donk had this bolt, not a small bolt a bloody big thing, from just before the start of his helmet through his japs eye.
There were gasps of "Fucking hell" and "Oh my god."
I wasn't pretty, it looked like it must have hurt like hell.
It certainly gave us and the rest of the pub something to talk about.
Near closing time, Donk came back from the toilets having pissed out the bottom hole, down his leg.
He confessed that he was on painkillers, he hadn't had sex since he'd had it done and that it hurt like hell.
To my knowledge none of the other lads followed Donks lead.

Rossy's Mam and Dad ran a couple of pubs over the years. They very kindly, inviting us all in. (no they weren't mad).
Paul's mam laid on food and really looked after us, his Dad left us in the bar, after the locals had been kicked out.
We never went too mad but always reached the "Can't drink any more level."

In a pub, on the outskirts of Middlesbrough, we'd had a really good night.
At 3 in the morning after mixing too many drinks, we all retired for the night, some sleeping under the bar, some under the tables.
I opted to sleep in the van in the secure carpark. An eight foot spiked fence kept up in and any potential thieves out.

I woke up in a bit of a daze.
I rubbed my eyes.
In front of me was a huge sign "South Cleveland Garages."
Somehow I had walked the 2 miles from the pub to the Trunk road garage.
"Shit."

I had never been sleep walking before in my life and now I had walked 2 miles in my boxer shorts.

I ran back, not really knowing the way.

I jogged as I thought that if the police turned up they wouldn't believe I had been sleep walking.

Eventually I got back to the pub.

The carpark fence was secure, the pub was locked up with no sign of life and no way in.

I knocked at the windows, nothing.

I could see bodies but none were alive.

I tried for 20mins, eventually waking the dead.

I laid off the drink for a while after that.

Mushrooms

Another story goes;-

On the 5th of November, one year, a large group of friends met around one of the lad's flats, they all had mushroom soup.

Not Heinz or Baxters but natural. It was magic.

After a short while some were seeing mould growing on the walls or people on the TV turning into elves with pointy ears.

Music played and colours appeared.

A film with Victoria Principle came on; her tits didn't just appear on the telly they came out of the screen. Some laughed and some got paranoid.

The friends went for a walk along the promenade, down the steps and took a walk on the lower prom next to the beach.

Rockets went off overhead, not really surprising it being bonfire night. This had differing effects.

Some whooped, laughing and dancing, while others were consumed by the ever increasing paranoia.

The group made its way into the woods.

The black darkness was broken by one lunatic who tried to set trees alight with sparklers.

This singular act brought back a few people from the brink of oblivion, others were not so lucky.

The group stayed together but all in their own little worlds as they drifted in and out of the real world.

They went into the Marine.

A strange place at the best of times but tonight the clientèle changed from humans to animals.

Wolves and cats. All very strange.

Back at the flat the come down was taking place. People crashed out.

Later a king-size bed shrunk to the size of a matchbox.

After 8 hours everything was back to normal. Whatever that is.

Stag nights

I've been on many nights out with the lads but a standout one was a joint stag weekend for Tash and Kev Elliot.

Scarborough was the venue, a place that we knew and loved. The charts were checked in the hope of surf, nothing all weekend.

We drove through in convoy 20 vans and cars; we parked at the North Bay near the swimming baths and Peasholme Park.

It was a bright sunny day so we made for the nearest pub.

The pub right on the corner was empty, the woman didn't quite know what to make of a large bunch of "scruffy" surfers.

All she knew was that the takings would be going through the roof.

All afternoon we sat and drank handcuffs and ball and chains were brought out and fixed to the "stags."

Rossy had the party jumper on.

Myself and A the B joined him.

The 3 headed 6 legged monster created chaos.

Talking with the lads, I commented that "I was never going to last the night drinking at this pace."

Keldy said that we should find a chemist and he would get us something that would make us last the night.

We emerged half cut from the pub and jumped on an open topped bus to the South bay.

God knows how we weren't arrested, a full upper deck of arses shown for miles down the seafront.

Into the town centre, we found a chemist; Do-Do tablets were purchased and consumed.

We continued on the pub crawl ending up at the Pickwick hotel.

Downstairs was full of bikers. We got some funny looks but A the B broke the ice ripping the piss out of a bunch of very large and hairy ones.

Their girlfriends ended up sitting with us, pool competitions continued and we even had some food.

Back at the swimming baths we changed.

Suited and booted we returned to the corner bar.

As we entered the woman behind the bar nearly fainted.

Her jaw nearly hit the floor.

"Come here all of you, let me have a good look. Oh my god, I don't believe it."
She seemed shocked.

We had a couple and then pub crawled into the town.

Back in the Pickwick the bikers commented on our attire.

Ok they just took the piss but we all had a good laugh.

We got in the nightclub no problem, the Do-Do tablets working.

We danced and sang and drank some more.

The rest of the night is a bit of a blur but I do remember wandering around
Peasholme Park at 4 in the morning, walking the Alice in Wonderland trail.

I found A the B walking the same trail.

He had a 3 foot ghetto blaster banging tunes out full blast and a stack of cans.

It was quite an effect listening to the music echo around the park, cracking cans.

In the morning there were a few bad heads. We had breakfast and set off for
Saltburn.

Once there, we were met by a few of the lads who couldn't make it to Scarborough.

We lured Tash onto the pier, where he was stripped, covered in syrup and feathers,
he was laughing as we said we were going to throw him off.

Seconds later his vans were removed, and he was launched off the pier 20 foot
into a cold North sea.

Looking back it would have been safer to take him to the very end, as it would
have been deeper.

But no-one could be bothered.

As I've said Tash wasn't a brilliant swimmer but he managed to get back to shore
O.K.

He was wet, sticky and still had lots of feathers all over. We All cheered from
the pier.

He was shouting something, about being a pack of bastards and was moaning
about something or other.

We adjourned to Rosie's.

Tom got married and I was Best Man.

He asked me "not to drop the rings."

It sort of, just happened, we chased them around and got them back. Phew.

It was a very nervous speech but I got a few laughs.

Tom's Mam bought me a very large Jameson's before hand which relaxed me a bit.

It turned out to be a good day and an excellent night.

Exodus

We all had our surfing adventures, exploring every corner of the globe.
Always returned to our Saltburn base with so many surfing stories.
Slowly we started to, sort of, "grow up."
Some were in long term relationships.
Houses and kids followed.
Some chased the dream, following their own endless summer.

Shorty had been to Australia a couple of times before.
He made his mind up early that Oz was the place for him.
He eventually settled down and started a family there with Kelly.
He's still living the dream.

Leggy, got a degree in surfing then worked down nearby Boulby potash mine.
He then followed Shorty to Australia via various Indonesian paradises.
People who didn't really know Leggy thought that he'd be back and settle down.
Leggy being Leggy got himself an opal mine...yeh, an opal mine in the outback.
60 feet down in a 3 foot shaft, digging with hydraulic jack hammers, bollock naked (cos of the heat) for months at a time.
I know.
Anyone else you'd think it was bullshit but this is Leggy we are talking about.
He uses the money to travel and surf for months at a time, living the dream.

Anth moved to London, travelled with work raising hell around Europe. Now he has a happy glow about him could be the lifestyle or something to do with where he's working. He returns to the Saltburn surf every now and again.

Donkey Al was last heard of living in the Cape Verdi islands.

Jeff Ridley moved due to ill health up to the Shetlands. Opened Sanday light railway. Regained full fitness, only to be stitched up by the council. Believed to be living in the middle of no-where in Yorkshire.

Kev, the adventurer, completed the first landrover expedition across the Himalaya's, toured the world and taught English in China for 6 months.
Can you imagine a class full of Chinese students following Kevs phrases:-
Now class say after me,"C'mon Boro" or "Gizza parmo, yah doyle" or "Wherez mi perple sheert, Mam."

Kev always returns home, usually has a smile on his face and doesn't look like a gorilla. (As photo).
Kev also rode from Lands End to John O'Groats and wrote a very entertaining book about his experience, "End to End."
And Keldy moved to Newquay, doing the thing that he loves best. Cooking and surfing. He is now a driving instructor.

As you have now realised, we didn't need an excuse to party.

When we did have an excuse, engagements, going away to foreign shores do's, birthdays etc we really pushed the boat out.

A favourite place to get away and have a party was at the Lion in at Blakey Ridge. It's an old fashioned place, low beams (Mind your head), real fires, good food and extended opening times.

Its situated miles away from anywhere high up on the North Yorkshire moors. Its got an extended carpark, so there's plenty of room for cars and vans, where the party always continued.

Fancy dress events happened every now and again, as well as, camping trips with the occasional BBQ.

Leggy always seemed to be dressed in womens clothes. St Trinians gear etc?!

House parties usually happen on the spur of the moment.

Around ours, Toms or Rossys.

Trampolines are meant for kids, not drunken adults.

Jumping off a shed roof, when very drunk isn't recommended.

We did have a few injuries, especially Ste with a nasty cut, suffered in an attempted flip.

The kids loved all that blood.

Rossy drank far too much wine, at one party. He eventually left at 3 in the morning.

Insisting that he was O.K. to peddle a few miles back home.

He fell off twice within 50 feet and ended up back at his place, sleeping in the shed because he had left his keys at ours.

Dod and Jackie, took over the Church fish and chip shop, in Saltburn for a number of years.

It was brilliant.

Word spread that it was a top chippie and people would turn up in their coach loads, to sample the best fish and chips around.

There was always a queue, no matter what day or what the weather.

HAWAIIAN ISLANDS

It is every surfers dream to go to the "Islands."

To follow in Captain Cook's footsteps and discover wondrous places and to surf some of the best waves in the world.

The seed was planted early with me as Hawaii five-o, with Steve McGarret, was a favourite on TV.

I still can hear Jack Lord say, "Book em Danno" as he solves yet another case.

Surfing featured in the titles and subconsciously I dreamed of one day surfing in Hawaii.

That could be total crap but that was what we were trying to do, the only problem for myself and Gill was the cost.

We had looked in the travel brochures, checked out the different islands.

We decided that we could go but would have to save had for 18 months. A very long wait.

When I had first started surfing I'd met a lot of really good, friendly people.

One person I'd known for a few years was Lee Crawford.

The first time I met him, he was pulling some brilliant skateboard tricks in the car park then he and his friend Turkey Mick went and ripped the waves apart.

I thought they were both talented bastards and then they came in the pub and joined in the drinking session.

A couple of years later, Lee married Andrea at Turtle beach, Oahu.

He came back but was so taken by the Hawaiin islands that they wanted to go back and settle down there.

I eventually got his address and wrote to the Aloha Punawai apart./hotel, Honolulu. (Cool address or what).

It turned out that Andrea was the manageress and Lee was the odd job man.

I wrote saying that we would be coming across in a year to 18 months.

The letter back said that they might miss us as they were waiting for a six month extension to their visa but didn't know.

I checked flight prices to Oahu again.

A few calls to Lee and Andrea made up our minds, they said that it would be possible to stay with them.

Bloody hell, we were going for 4 weeks, we had bought our plane tickets coming back 23rd December. The dream was becoming reality.

After Bali and a couple of other holidays we thought that we were well practised travellers.

We boarded the plane at Manchester, bound for Chicago where we'd have an overnight stop then on to Oahu.

The plane was packed with Americans. All with have a nice day accents.

O.K. but after a while it got right on my tits.

The drinks were free and we took full advantage, through the 8 1/2 hour flight. Wouldn't you?

Thankfully Gill was O.K. on this flight, no repeat of the Bali experience.

At Chicago's O'Hare airport, we booked into the Chelsea motel in Des Plaines, a suburb.

The room turned out to be a bit dossy but for one night it didn't matter.

We dumped our bags and headed for K-Mart, which we had passed in the taxi.

It was quite warm so we went for a walk.

We walked the half mile to the store, not thinking anything as cars cruised by slowing down then speeding off.

No-one, not even a dog was on the streets.

We bought a few things and checked out places to eat, we ended up in Burger King. Very American.

We got talking to a local, he couldn't believe we were walking.

All we got out of him was "Your kidding me."

No mate we're not.

He went on to tell us that less than a mile away were the Projects, blocks of houses containing prison fodder.

People mixed up with drugs, prostitution and murder.

We explained that Saltburn was a smaller version of this. (Only kidding). I wanted to go for a look but Gill didn't for some reason, can't think why.

Needless to say we got a taxi back.

We crashed out knackered by booze and travelling.

We woke 12 hours later, then a mad rush back to the airport.

Got the taxi to terminal 5, phew still a bit of time to spare.

Looked at the huge departures board.

It turned out that we were in the wrong terminal.

Gill started to get worried, I was doing the "We'll make it, no problem." But inside I was going fucking hell, fucking hell."

We got to terminal 3 and ran to the check-in desk. They said because we were late we'd have to go to gate K-16 to be seated.

We ran again.

We waited while people boarded.

Gill at this stage was not too chuffed to say the least. The stress levels were through the roof.

We went to the desk the stewardess smiled and gave us our seat tickets. 6D and 6G.

Gill wasn't over pleased when she said "Have a nice flight."

"Have a nice flight, were not even sitting together!"

Almost in tears, we boarded.

Our luck then changed.

We were shown into business class, 6D and 6G turned out to be in the middle row and next to each other.

Two huge leather armchairs.

I kept expecting to be turfed out back to economy.

"It's been a terrible mistake, sorry sir." It never happened.

We had struck lucky again.

Our stewardess gave us champagne, Gill smiled, stress what stress.

The flight was a drink fuelled pleasure ride, the best flight ever.

We stepped off the plane into brilliant sunshine, Lee met us within yards of getting into the airport.

Andrea was waiting in the car with friends boys, Sean and Ian.

We drove to the apartments in Saratoga Road, dropped the bags off and went straight to Waikiki beach.

The sand was warm, three foot surf gently caressed the shore, Diamond Head in the distance, Hawaiian music drifting out from a hotel bar.

We'd made it.

Lee and Andrea took the boys on a catamaran ride while we started to explore.

We found loads of surf shops with beautiful boards, packed full of surf clothing.

We passed by "the Duke's" statue, a surfing icon, checked out loads of boards chained up next to the police station.

We had something to eat, stayed up until the early hours with Lee and Andrea drinking and talking. Absolutely knackered at the end of the day, we crashed.

Over the next few days we hired boards and surfed local Waikiki breaks No3's, Pops and Canoes.

It was small but perfect waves, surfing in board shorts in bath water temperature was a pleasure. There were a lot of people in the water, but it was no bother catching waves.

189

Lee took us to an unforgettable place, Hanauma bay beach park. On the way we stopped for crab sticks, I thought Lee wanted a snack.

We went snorkelling.

Waist deep in water we were surrounded by loads of fish, big fish.

We handed the masks over to Gill and Andrea.

Lee got the crab sticks out and we both tore strips off them and threw them behind the lasses.

They came out screaming, hundreds of fish were surrounding them searching for any scraps, some jumping clean out of the water. I nearly pissed myself laughing.

Later, we walked around the bay and found a place called the toilet bowl, a pool whose level rises and falls 8 feet with each wave.

It sucked you down then blasted you up at speed. A mini blow hole, excellent fun.

We had a lazy day sunbathing and swimming.

Picnic on the beach with a few beers. I could feel myself really unwinding.

We wanted to see more of Oahu, so we hired a car for the week.

Our first port of call was, of course, the North shore.

We travelled through field after field of pineapples along the Kam highway. It took an hour to cross the island.

We drove from Haleiwa to Turtle bay.

We stopped every where to check places out, at one spot lee threw out his arm and declared "this is Pipeline."

"Piss off, that's not Pipeline."

It was a lovely bit of beach, you could see fingers of coral just below the flat calm surface of the sea.

In my mind Pipeline was the old spice advert, the gnarly fierce huge barrel of a wave, grinding allcomers into oblivion.

Here I was travelled nearly half way around the world and it was flat.

Lee said "Just you wait and see."

We stopped at Wiamea bay.

I had seen it on so many videos, it seemed very familiar. The beach, the rocks, the shape of the coastline and the Catholic church with its tower which looks over the bay.

Even when its flat it is an awesome place.

We drove up above Wiamea to Pu'u o Mahuka Heiau, a religious site with a ruined temple overlooking the bay.

We found fruit offerings and leaves pushed into the ruined walls.

Andrea told us that if you wrap a stone in a tea leaf and place it in the wall then your wish would come true.

Not really convinced we all found a stone wrapped it up in a tea leaf and wished keeping the wishes secret.

My wish was to surf Wiamea bay one day... (always be careful what you wish for).

We continued on. At Turtle bay, Lee showed us where he and Andrea were married. Later, he showed us the photos. Andrea in a white wedding dress and Lee in his board shorts.

The next day, back at the North shore, a small swell had arrived.

We hired boards, mine was a battered 9'7".

We searched for some surf, it came at a place called Laniakea or Lannies, it was only 4ft but the long right handers were irrisistable.

As we paddled out, it started to rain, hot rain.

A rainbow lit up the rocks and beach.

Huge sea turtles swam by and I caught what I thought were really brilliant North shore waves.

O.K. I cruised them while Lee was tearing them to bits.

A huge local surfer shouted over to me, "Hey howdy" followed by some other words that I didn't quite hear cos of the noise from the surf.

I paddled over "alright, how you doing?"

This giant of a man then went on a bit of a rant about Americans coming over here and stealing all the waves then he called me a howlie and told me in no uncertain terms to go home.

I sat and smiled and explained that I'm English not American and if ever he came over he would be welcome in any of our breaks. He would have to bring his own 6mm wetsuit though as I doubted we would have anything that large.

He shook his head and said that "he didn't do wetsuits",

Then he a bit laughed said something which I didn't catch and caught the next wave.

I think I got away with it.

I later found out that a howlie is a mythical creature without a soul, most tourists / white people are called this by Hawaiians a kind of racist comment. Each to their own.

At the end of the day, though ,we both came out with that surfed out buzz.

My hired board was O.K. but I needed a board of my own.

We trawled around loads of surf shops over the next few days in search of a special board. The choice was overwhelming.

Eventually I found a Blue Hawaii 9' 1" longboard shaped by Ernie Tanaka, its one of those boards that just looks and feels right.

I bought it and couldn't wait to get it in the water.

Gill and I got up early one morning and headed for the North shore, Lee gave us directions to a beach break (ideal for soft wipe outs) near Pipeline called Pupukea or Ehukia beach.

We surfed for a couple of hours taking turns to ride the new board.

The surf was 6 foot but really mellow and an easy paddle out.

After quite a few wipeouts we both started to get the hang of it. Gill daring to go right into the teeth of waves and getting away with it. We both encouraged each other.

Knackered we went for something to eat at the Haleiwa cafe, a really cool surfers place.

We ordered breakfast.

What came was a mountain of food, bacon, sausage, eggs (fried and scrambled), mushrooms, potato things? and then pancakes with syrup and loads of coffee.

Fit to bust we left, we went to Wiamea bay and sunbathed. Both fell asleep. Gill got sunburned.

We went back to the car only to see the keys in the ignition and the doors locked. We looked at each other. "Oh fuck."

Luckily we found a lifeguard who got in using a bendy piece of steel, it cost us 5 litres of pineapple juice but was worth it.

We had a drive around and got back evening time, Gill wasn't feeling too good, so we had an early night.

The next day was a bit of a right off, as Gill was still feeling a bit dodgy, lots of sun and pancakes don't mix.

I went out and got some tourist leaflets about the other islands. We decided that we would have a mini tour and visit Maui, Kauai and the Big island Hawaii.

Lee woke me up, early.

Just phoned the surfline and the North shore is getting some descent waves through do you fancy it.

I looked at Gill, (should I stay or should I go)... Gill said what are you waiting for, go on go.

We arrived at Haleiwa, waves a bit mushy, we decided Sunset beach would be better (not that I had much of a clue where we were going).

Lee said what about here? Here was Rocky point, there were rights and lefts going off 6-8ft.

It turned out to be onto shallow reef. Funny that being a reef break, Rocky point.

I was starting to have second thoughts but Lee was so enthusiastic.

After an easy paddle out I tried to pick my spot. I sat and watched as lee and five or six others made it look so easy.

I got into the line up and paddled for a wave. It looked so slow but was super fast, I managed the bottom turn but was mugged at the bottom of the wave. I was soon getting tumbled over and over.

Back in the line up, I caught my breath and paddled again.

Take off, bottom turn then held my board into the face.

The power and speed of this medium size wave was brilliant.

My confidence started to build.

My wipeouts far out numbered my rides, but I was happy.

Lee was ripping, months of surfing everyday in near perfect conditions had pushed him to another level.

After getting changed, we went to Sunset beach to watch the pros take part in one of the Triple Crown events then back to Ehukai where the Oxbow longboard competition was happening.

Watching the pros rip the place to bits in a graceful balletic manner was brilliant to see close up.

The lads on the longboards, were pulling every trick and move in the book and a few new ones thrown in for good luck.

It was a pleasure watching these natural surfers.

Lee spotted one of my long time heroes, Greg "Da Bull" Noll.
I had a photo with him and was really in awe of this surfing legend.

He'd obviously had a few pies over the years, he was a big bloke in every
dimension. It was a pleasure meeting him.

On the way back to Waikiki we took a bit of a diversion down the East coast.
Lee showed me a very posh estate near Waimanalo beach.
We sneaked around a corner I asked "What the fuck are we doing?"
He pointed saying "don't you recognise this place."
Just as I started to say no, the house and gardens where "Magnum" lived came
into view.
Someone's private estate very beautiful. We didn't stay too long just in case the
current owners had dobermans.

Wiamea bay

The night before was spent in the Hard Rock cafe, pigging out on nachos,
guacamole, burgers and lots of beer. We'd all returned to Lee and Andreas place
and drank Miller Lite well into the morning.
It had turned colder and it was raining.
Lee said that we might get some swell from this.
I thought nothing of it.
I had an untroubled sleep.

Lee had phoned the surf line very early.

He came in and asked if I wanted to surf Waimea, he said it was a good 8 foot with a light offshore wind and it was a beautiful day.

We all got up quickly and packed loads of stuff for a day at Waimea bay. Carefully strapping the boards to the car roof.

My mind was racing, I'd wish wed had a quieter night, my guts were churning.

I didn't know whether this was down to the food, the beer or the thought of surfing Wiamea.

Normally quiet a laid back positive person, I was turning very panicky.

Maybe I knew what was coming.

I was thinking far too much, would I get stuck in the shore break?

Would I get trapped beneath the waves in one of Wiamea's caves?

I was psyching myself out. I was getting paranoid. I didn't want to make a complete prat of myself.

All my surfing life was building towards this moment, small Waimea.

8 foot, I could handle that no problem.

The drive to the North shore seemed a long one, I was now in a cold sweat.

This is what real fear is about. I was shitting myself.

The thought "Was I afraid to die" popped into my head.

"Fucking hell, yes" was my answer to myself.

My first sight of the swell did nothing to calm me down.

The closer we got the more convinced I became, that Waimea was a step too far and I would have to spend the day watching from the beach.

196

As we turned into the bay, I could see the heavy shore break dumping onto the beach.

I'd seen it in so many videos I knew it well.

Lines of surf came from over the horizon.

Big waves, not the 8 foot Lee had mentioned.

Apparently the Hawaiians measure waves from the back, there were sets of 14 feet and bigger.

"No fucking way was I going out in that, not a fucking chance."

I was now talking out loud, not just in my head.

We parked up and unloaded the gear.

Lee was buzzing, "C'mon lets go before the pros get all the waves."

I said I'd watch for a bit, my confidence shattered into a million pieces.

Fear ravaged me, not just the oh shit type of fear but the if I go out there I'm going to die type.

I watched as Lee battled through the shore break and out into the channel.

I helped the lasses set up on the beach for the day.

I paced around the shoreline like a father paces before the birth of his child.

I tried to convince myself that I could do this.

I watched dark threatening sets slowly enter the bay.

Slow, monster waves majestically formed, perfect.

Fine plumes of white spray erupted high into the air.

They broke seemingly in slow motion.

Dare devils, "proper surfers" had rides of their lives.

This wasn't, by Waimea standards, close to a big day, it was more a fun day, for most.

It was more serious for me.

A helicopter buzzed in over the line up, a photographer leaning out of the door.

Gill broke my trance by saying, "Are you going in? Its a shame not to, we've come all this way..."

I waxed my board.

Thoughts racing through my head.

If I make it past the beach break I'd be happy.

I tied my board shorts a bit tighter, kissed Gill and said "Fuck it lets go", through gritted teeth.

I picked up my board and ran into the surf.

I dived onto my board and paddled as though my life depended on it.

I focused my thoughts, my actions, everything to break through the dumping shorebreak.

Jon Metcalfe

I paddled, I duck dived, I battled.
Within minutes I'd got through the shore break and into the channel.
I breathed a sigh of relief. At least I had made it out.
A large set rolled in, I knew I'd be O.K. in the channel.
I sat on my board and took it all in.
People on the beach were tiny ants, the church was a good point to fix your position as was the lifeguard tower.
I noticed 2 surfers paddling for one of the biggest waves of the day, one backed off the other paddled hard and got to his feet,
The slow giant of a wave now seemed very fast.
The surfer began to freefall, the lip following close behind.
He looked to get an edge in but he just fell. His arms above and behind him, trying to keep balanced.
He hit the bottom and was smashed by the lip.
The volume of water and the force this surfer was being pounded by was frighteningly awesome.
Hundreds of yards away, I counted the seconds waiting for him to surface.
10 seconds, 20 seconds nothing, after 30 seconds I saw a board pop up... Followed by Lee.
I paddled over, "Are you O.K.?"
He looked at me saying "fucking hell, that was faster than I thought", then he turned and paddled back outside. He encouraged me into the line up.
About a dozen other surfers sat waiting for the next set. No-one said much.
Another dark set appeared on the horizon, everyone turned and paddled.
I paddled like hell after them, not wanting to be caught inside.
As I paddled up the face of the first wave, my balls were in my throat.
This wasn't a wave, it was a solid wall of water, a fucking mountain.
I paddled harder.
Over the top and down the steep backside.
Adrenaline, now pumping fast through my body.
I saw the next wave slightly bigger.
Surfers were turning their boards and paddling in the other direction, ready for a rollercoaster ride.
I was careful not to get in anyone's way and very keen to make progress until I was safely outside.
The sound of the waves breaking will stay with me forever.
A thunderous, rumbling followed by a crashing, so loud, so powerful.
As I sat on my board, safe outside I felt completely isolated from everyone else and the world.

Was this what surfing is all about, me against the sea? The fun was gone. This was survival.

I watched as pros and experienced surfers caught waves, I tried to figure out the best place to take off.

I thought I'd got it sussed?!

I watched a set come in and began to paddle for the first wave. I paddled like a madman, no-one else paddled. I felt myself being sucked up by the wave, the island seemed to be getting sucked in as well.

The wave rolled by as I slid off the back.

The wave was faster than I had thought my paddling didn't get anywhere near the speed to catch it.

Now out of position, I turned my board and paddled back out, praying not to get sucked over the falls backwards.

After an unnerving paddle I was sat outside again.

I was getting tired not so much physically but mentally.

I made up my mind to catch one wave and call it a day.

It was easier said than done, sets came and went.

I paddled and either pulled out after looking down a very large drop or seeing someone else on the wave.

I'd been in the water 2 hours and caught nothing. Those hours seemed like a lifetime.

I watched another set rolling in.

The first wave, I was in the wrong position but the second I was just about right.

I grabbed large handfuls of water, I was committed, no backing out,

"This is it" I thought.

Paddling fast and steady. I didn't look back. I was fully focused.

I felt myself being sucked up and up...then I was being thrown forward.

"Shiiiitttt", I was on a wave at Waimea bay,

"Ohhhhh, shiiiiitttt."

I got to my feet (not too quickly), I held a rail, I kept crouched low, hoping my speed would out run any white water monster behind.

I stood and turned the board slightly right, full speed.

"Fuck this was fast."

I was to scared to breathe..

I was now flying along the face of the wave, in control, just.

Close behind I heard what I can only describe as a flat boom.

I ducked expecting to be wiped out, I straightened out, white water engulfed me.

I'd seen it on the Waimea videos, just when you think you've done the hard work you get crushed.

I kept going, bumping along the face at high speed.

I crouched again, my legs were suddenly chopped away by the power of the white water.

I was flipped and wiped out almost immediately.

I surfaced within seconds and pulled the board back to me.

I crawled on board and started paddling in. Not vaguely tempted to paddle back out again.

The shore break was unforgiving , it dumped me on the sand and then dumped me again.

I was so glad to make it back to the beach.

My legs shook, my body shook...

For a few minutes I just sat. I was buzzing, adrenaline coursing through my veins.

I found Lee with the lasses sunbathing.

Gills first words were "Did you manage to get out there and did you catch many waves?"

I said "I was the one out there, who was shitting himself and yes I did catch one wave."

I would like to say that I was prepared for Wiamea, I wasn't.

I would like to say that I caught a massive wave and ripped. I didn't.

Respect to all who enter the water at this legendary place. For the few who ride it on the biggest days, double respect, whatever that is.

I can honestly say that I caught one wave in 2 hours and that I scared myself stupid.

To surf any wave I believe you have to be committed 100%, on my Waimea day I wasn't even close.

Like I said be careful what you wish for.

After recovering on the beach and soaking up the sun, we had something to eat nearby.

Lee was up for another Waimea session, I talked him into the safer option at Ehukia beach, a break that I was getting to love..

I really enjoyed the next couple of hours in the surf.

It was a relief to be familiar with a break. Yes I still had wipeouts but as I bounced off the sandy bottom, I knew that I'd be paddling back out for another wave.

In the next few days we did some tourist stuff.

We climbed to the top of Diamond Head, I wish I had taken a torch as the last bit of the climb was through a narrow tunnel then up a spiral staircase. All in complete darkness. It was knackering but well worth the effort.

We visited Pearl Harbour, I was amazed at the number of Japanese tourists taking pictures of anything that moved.

We went body surfing at Sandy beach, Gill put her full swimming costume on. As we paddled furiously into the barrelling beach break, the incoming wave picks you up and if you do a superman impression you get a very fast barrel ride.

Brilliant fun until the wipeout when you are tumbled into the soft sand then done over. Gill was held underwater a couple of times, as her bathing costume had filled with sand weighing her down. Very scary for her at the time. A beautiful but dangerous place.

To give Lee and Andrea a bit of space and to extend our adventure, we booked a 3 island trip.

Over a week, we would visit Maui, Hawaii, (the Big island) and Kauii.

Maui was only a 25 minute flight. On arrival we drove to Wailea, where we were staying. We dropped the bags and searched for surf.

We found a 4 foot wave at Lahaina, which turned out to be a bit disappointing.

We searched the other side of the island and found Hookipa big and messy with loads of rocks, didn't fancy being smashed to pieces.

We looked at the map and decided to drive up to the summit of Haleakala. It seemed like a good idea at the time but it turned out to be a driving nightmare.

The most amount of bends I've ever driven up, it really did your head in. Excellent views from the top over to the coast and into the islands large crater.

At the top it was a bit like a moonscape and cold because of the altitude.

There was an observatory up there but not open to tourists.

The drive back was very, very long and windey.

Over the next day or two we toured around the spectacular "Valley Isle" there is so much to see and we had such a short time to cram everything into.

Next we visited Kauai, the Garden Isle.

We stopped in Wailua, in a hotel across the road from Coco palms. Elvis got married there in Blue Hawaii, so we were told.

Coco Palms break itself was a messy 6 foot.

We drove to Ke"e on the North shore, the rain came down and we saw some fantastic rainbows.

Went in the water at Hanalei.

It was only 4 foot but it was a long barrelling wave that seem to reform in three different places.

Later we checked out Kauai's Waimea. A place where Captain Cook had first landed. It looked a bit ramshackled.

The island, at the time of our visit, was just recovering from a recent hurricane the devastation was still there for us to see.

Hawaii, the Big island, was my favourite place to visit.

There was plenty of volcanic activity.

Old lava flows, huge craters still steaming, large rocks glowing red hot, lava tubes.

We drove through rainforests and high alpine landscapes.

We stopped everywhere, getting out of the car to explore.

We stopped in both Hilo and Kona both could do with a bit of modernisation. Hilo definitely had a 50's feel.

We visited Kealakekua bay where Captain Cook was killed in 1779.

I was a bit disappointed. There were so many beautiful locations and he ended up here on a rater plain bay. There is a small monument dedicated to him but nothing special.

It was a whistle stop tour but I'm so glad we made the effort.

It would have been good if we had more time on each island.

Maybe next time, after the lottery win.

We returned to Oahu and spent loads of time in the surf and just kicking back with Lee and Andrea.

We watched the Christmas parades and got lost in the crowds.

We had a last visit to the North shore.

It was cold, overcast but the surf was pumping in.

We sat and watched people get eaten at big Pipeline.

A 20 foot plus, perfect barrelling wave was hypnotic. There were loads of broken boards that day.

Was I tempted to go in?

Don't be bloody daft...no chance.

After almost a month in the Islands it was nearly time to get back home.

With only hours to spare before our flight we both had our last surf sessions at Waikiki beach.

Sat out back waiting for waves gave me time to reflect.

We'd crammed so much in but leaving would be so hard.

After we had surfed Gill just looked at me and said "I suppose that's it then."

That gutted feeling was descending.

We walked to a "Local Motion" surf shop nearby. They had agreed to bubble wrap and box the board for the journey.

My beautiful board was now a ten foot cardboard box.

After picking up our cases, Lee and Andrea took us to the airport. The board tied to the roof with some washing line.

We drove very carefully.

At the airport we said our goodbyes, it was really difficult, Lee and Andrea had made us so welcome.

It was getting harder to leave, with tears in our eyes we made our way through to customs.

The customs men were brilliant asking all about my board, where we had surfed and when we were coming back again.

We found out that the cases and board would be taken all the way and that we would be reunited at Manchester airport, where we had arranged for Gills brother to pick us up.

Before that we were having a full day in Chicago.

The plane journey to Chicago was uneventful. We arrived at some unearthly hour.

When the plane door opened a cold draft came through the plane.

Both myself and Gill looked at each other in our summer clothes. Shorts seemed a good idea in Hawaii but now, now it was -3C.

Warmer clothes were needed and soon. We jumped onto the train into the city centre.

We stood out like sore thumbs, not just because of our clothes but because we were the only white people on board.

All the locals were wrapped up in woolly hats gloves and thick jackets.

As we walked from the station we saw people ice skating, on an outside ice rink. Most of the shops were still closed, we spotted a McDonalds and sought sanctuary there.

Inside the heating was full blast, we ate and drank lots of coffee.

We waited for the shops to open.

We made a run for it back out in the cold to the nearest department store.

We bought warm clothes, paid for them, then went back in the changing room and got dressed.

Much to the amusement of a couple of shop assistants who were slightly inquisitive about why we were walking around in shorts on such a cold day.

The rest of the day was spent sight seeing, buying more Christmas presents and avoiding tramps which seemed to make a beeline for us for "some change."

At first the polite "No" worked but by the end of the day it had descended to "Nah fuck off."

We had a few drinks and watched brain numbing films on the plane journey back to Manchester.

We both just wanted to get home.

As we got off the plane it was overcast and raining.

At least we will be getting home soon, I thought.

Gill phoned her brother, as I picked up the cases and ten foot box.

A customs woman stopped me and asked loads of questions, it turned out that she was planning a trip to Hawaii.

She undercharged me for the tax on the board and we moved through into the arrivals.

Gill told me that her brother wasn't coming to pick us up, he'd been called into work.

No problem, we'd get a coach home.

Oh no you wont, can't have a ten foot box on here.

Train, this would involve getting a shuttle and then train from Victoria to Darlington.

Sorry son can't have a ten foot box on here. Said the shuttle driver.

Taxi to Victoria train station.

No chance.

O.K. last resort hire a car.

No chance we had both been drinking.

We were well and truly screwed...

I tried the shuttle train driver and the conductor again. I told them we'd been to Hawaii and this was our only way to get home. Luckily they let us on.

We bought tickets from the airport to Darlington, we would have ten minutes to wait before our train.

We got off in Victoria station, cases, bags and a ten foot box.

We found out that our train was waiting on the furthest platform away, platform 13...brilliant.

We struggled up stairs, ran as best we could.

Gill was starting to get a bit frustrated, I told her to get on the train and try to hold it.

She ran ahead case wheeling behind her.

The last flight of stairs to the platform was a nightmare, bags flew, the case banged and the box was just a pain in the arse.

As I got to the train, the conductor stopped me. "sorry son you can't bring that on here."

Gill came out, the driver came out, we had a short discussion.
It was decided we could come on board and hold it in place on the parcel shelf.
After a very long journey home, Gill's Mam and Dad met us at the station.
Gill got a lift back to their house with the bags and cases.
I walked the ¾'s of a mile with my 10 foot box.

It was a week later when I rode the board at Saltburn.
Had all the trouble been worth it...damn right it had.

LIFE CHANGES

Life changing things started to happen for myself and Gill.
James and then Laura, my kids, came along.

James and Laura
I was lucky enough to be present at the birth of both James and Laura, my kids.
The greatest feeling in the world, is when you hold your kids for the first time, nothing gets close.

O.K. what's this got to do with surfing?
Well, both the kids arrived home after a couple of days in hospital.
Once home, the video (the older version of a DVD) of Big Wednesday was played for them, as well as, assorted longboard videos.
They were both introduced to surfing very early.
I'm half expecting the NSPCC around.

At 2, James had a paddle around on a board at "Spanish left" Tenerife.

This was memorable for me.
As I pushed James around on the board, I stood on a sea urchin.
Its spines were to say the least quite painful.
I didn't like to cry in front of a two year old, so I waited until I was on the beach.

Surfing took a back seat while the kids were small, but I still managed to get in now and again.
Who could resist the calling from the waves?

We would take it in turns to get up and look after the kids during the night. Sometimes putting the kids in the pushchair and wandering down to the beach. It was a knackering time but from our upstairs windows you could check the surf out.

When everyone was settled and Gill took over, I would disappear for a dawn patrol.

After even the shortest session you felt ready for anything.

Slowly, more and more of the people we knew had kids.

The next generation of surfers was coming.

Dangerous and Andrea, Tom and Leigh, Rossy and Lorraine, Tash and Mel, Dod and Jackie, Kev and Julie, Wils and Vic, Gary and Christine, Shorty and Kelly, Anth and Sarah, Kev E and Sue (Pollard), Lee and Andrea, all had kids. There are obviously loads more, the list is endless.

The kids provided a good excuse to get away for weekends and to have a laugh. We got organised.

Vans, caravans and tents. Footballs, toys and always loads of beer. We were already BBQ experts, so food was no problem.

A lot of the time was spent near the coast, so if there was any chance of surf then we'd be there.

It was a special time for everyone.

James, my son, started surfing early.

At five years old, he rode his first wave, on the second attempt. I don't know where he got that from.

Laura, my daughter, loves the sea and swims like a fish. She's into boogie boarding at the minute, I can't wait until she's riding her own board.

I've already told her, no surfer boyfriends.

The kids are so enthusiastic and that rubs off on me.

"Can we go surfing Dad?"

"Lets go and check out the waves."

"Lets go"

And if your not awake then there's the usual "Pile on Dad...aaaagggghhhh."
There are plenty of the other lads, who can be seen regularly passing on their experience and knowledge to the next generation.

WIPEOUTS

Why do wipeouts stay with us, in our thoughts and dreams?

Is it that fear of a close to death experience or just making a complete arse out of yourself?

Why do seconds seem like hours when your in freefall?

I'm sure that there's a scientific explanation but that's not what this is about.

Wipeouts mean that you are in there trying. It only requires you to be a fraction out of position or just caught out by a rogue wave.

Every surfer has them.

I believe if they don't kill you, it makes you a stronger surfer, mentality.

Here are my favourite nightmares.

EARLY DAYS AT SALTBURN WIPEOUT

It was one of those cold crisp winter days when everyone was either wrapped up with a million layers on or in the pub in front of the fire.

The surf was only 3-4 foot powerful and messy, peaks everywhere loads of white water, the salt in the air burnt your eyes.

There was the occasional better set but it was a long time coming.

Looking back we must have been desperate for a wave.

We got some strange looks from all the people not brave enough to venture out.

We paddled out on the Marske side of the pier as the waves looked slightly better.

Tom and Jeff caught early waves, myself, Tash and Ste seemed to take an age to get out back.

My first wave of the day, I paddled like hell, bounced about a bit got to my feet and rode it all the way into the beach. Not bad.

As I paddled out I caught sight of tom paddling for a wave far to my left hand side a lot further out.

I continued to battle the white water, 3 paddles forward 2 back.

Tom had caught his wave and was cruising, I felt sure he'd seen me, I kept paddling .

He was getting closer so I gave him a shout,

Now in the impact zone, Tom turned his head and saw me,

The look on his face was a picture.

It was a, shit, what the fuck are you doing there, shocked look.

He bailed out over the back of the wave but unfortunately kicked his board straight towards me.

It happened that fast I had no time to react.

Time slowed, Toms board hit my cheek just below my eye. I felt the explosion, my head recoiled.

The burning sensation was immediate.

For a couple of seconds the lights just went out.

The cold water soon brought me back to reality.

I took the next wave in.

There seemed to be blood everywhere, I held my skin in place as I body boarded back.

I walked up the beach my eye closing by the second, blood dripping in big blobs.

As I reached the top step, a lass grabbed me saying that she was a first aider and she'd seen what had happened.

From time to time a first aid caravan would set up usually for the tourists...now I was in it dripping seawater and blood.

She said things like "Ooh that looks nasty" and "I think you might need stitches in that."

That wasn't really what I wanted to hear.

She dowsed me with TCP, "aaaaagggghhhh, fucking hell", I nearly hit the roof, she cleaned the wound and put on butterfly plasters.

As she was writing out the medical form she asked loads of questions.

She wrote on the form which I was to take to the hospital, cause of injury from surfing, I liked that bit.

Tom stopped by "sorry about that, didn't see you."

My fault shouldn't have been in the way I said, followed by a two fingered gesture.

He handed me a can of lager from the van.

"Ahh thats much better" I said, as I gulped a large mouthful.

The first aider lass just shook her head as we left, shouting "you should really get stitches."

Later my eye closed up completely and went all colours of the rainbow, (it was weird looking at your eye when the white bits all red).

I did get a lot of sympathy, for a couple of minutes followed by piss taking.

I wouldn't have expected anything else.

POINT / PENNY'S SALTBURN WIPEOUT

Friday night had started with a pub crawl around Middlesbrough's finest pubs with a few loony mates from work, Sammy, Big Rob and Geordie Jim.

We weren't the posing types wearing the right labels and drinking only the trendiest bottles of lager.

As I'm sure you've already guessed we were just out for a laugh.

On went the false beards and the glow in the dark eyes, people just didn't know how to take us, it was brilliant.

We ended up in the Boro's best night club, the Madison, (sadly gone).

The bouncers took one look shook their heads and waved us in.

We danced and drank then drank some more...to say it was a very heavy, but entertaining, night was an underestimation.

Paula, Sammys girlfriend, at the time, apparently found me outside slumped by a BHS window.

I couldn't even remember if I'd heard Herb Albert "This guy's in love", always one of the last records.

She put me in a taxi and told the driver to take me to Saltburn carpark.

It was after 3 a.m.

I paid the driver and stood sobering up, lashed by wind and rain.

I listening to the pounding surf.

I crashed out in the back of Tom's van.

Dawn and I'm stunned back into reality by Shorty opening the van door.

"Check this out" he said, staring at the point.

Six of us stood under the threatening grey skies.

The conversation went:-

What do you recon?

The beach is too big and messy,

6ft outside point, maybe bigger...did you see that barrel.

Come on lets go...

And that was it, no time to think.

It was get up and go.

We all changed quickly and walked towards Huntcliff, the Ship and the channel for the paddle out.

Six figures on a deserted beach.

It was clear, as we got closer, that the 6 ft waves were a lot bigger.

Big and gnarly.

As we paddled through the channel I can honestly say that I felt like shite.

Not much sleep, no food, too much beer and vodka.

I was the last one out, I watched Shorty drop down a huge face bottom turn then tuck for a barrel.

He and the wave roared past.

Leggy was on a bigger peak away to my left, with his wide stance he was unmistakable.

I didn't see the rest of them until later in the carpark.

Big sets were rolling in, I paddled out over them.

I looked around another set was looming.

I sat, spun my board around and paddled.

My world went into slow motion, I was looking down on myself shouting "Nooooooo, not this one" but I didn't hear.

I paddled hard, then in mid paddle I stopped and looked over my shoulder, the wave sucked me up.

The lip seemed to jack up above me, I tried to get to my feet.

The wave kicked.

I was free falling, slow motion, backwards.

I saw the wave, dark grey but the lip brilliant white.

I crashed and the wave swallowed me, no time for a last breath,

I was in the tumble dryer.

Flung around and around, "When's this going to end," I thought.

Over and over, head over heels,

I didn't know which way was up, I managed a couple of strokes and felt myself being sucked backwards, deeper down.

I started to relax, tumbled again.

Seconds lasting minutes.

This was getting very weird.

I waited for the bright light, it never came. A million thoughts filled my head.

I saw the Evening Gazette headlines

"SURFER DIES AT SALTBURN..."

Survival mode finally kicked in.

I felt for my leash and literally climbed it hoping it would lead to safety.

I broke the surface took a deep breath, then was hammered back down again by another freight train wave in the set.

This time it was a shorter hold down, I came up like a drowning rat, praying for another breath.

I pulled on my leash, my board glided over to me, exhausted I climbed on board.

I paddled out and looked around, no-one, was in sight.

Is this how surfing is meant to be just you and the sea?

I paddled some more, the carpark and pier seemed so distant.

Dark shapes appeared on the horizon, another set.

My instinctive plan, get the first wave in.

No mistakes this time I paddled, held the rail on the drop and rode it for what seemed ages. I bounced around, belly boarding into the beach.

I got out and sat on the rocks in front of the Ship pub.

I shook more with relief, the adrenalin buzzing through my veins.

Writing this now brings it all back. The hairs on the back of my neck are standing up. The image of this wipeout is seared on my brain forever.
It still scares the shit out of me but we laugh and start all over again.
One more mile on my thousand mile surfers stare.
I went back in the water with Tom and Shorty after we'd had some food at Rosie's.
The afternoon session was nothing to write home about.
The wind was cross shore and it was just messy but it was good to get back in the water.
That night we ended up in the Rosie's then the Marine, no matter how much I drank I stayed completely sober.
Sleep was next to impossible.
When it did come I was flung back into a nightmare scenario falling down the faces of waves held down waking in a sweat. I knew this had been a close one.

Days after, I was still thinking about the wipe out so in a bit of a drunken daze, I wrote a poem about it, (yes, I know what your thinking, poem, must have been drinking far too much etc):

Early morning in the dew,
Ten foot glass in front of you,
Grab your board and run down the track,
Then paddle hard through the sets, out back

The first wave of the day,
Paddle, up, and on your way,
Just hold that line against the wall,
The wave jacks up, barrels then falls
Wipe out, washer dried,
Headlines flash, how a surfer died,
Thinking how to cheat this drowning death,
Battling upwards to catch a breath.

Explode the surface, gulp the air,
Scramble on the board, taking care,
Ride the white water into the bay,
Collapse on the beach, what a day.

S'LAND WIPEOUT

S'land is a beautiful, historic, dangerous place.

It's without doubt a world class destination, with 3 break main breaks.

I had ridden the harbour break, when it was small to medium, a couple of times and thought it to be slow, mellow but with a lot of power.

Today, was different.

As myself and Tom drove down the wet narrow cobbled streets, we were greeted by the Cove going off its tits, big and powerful.

Light offshore winds and no-one else around.

Tom did his usual trick, calling it 4 foot when it was a lot bigger, nearer 10 foot.

I played the game.

I'm not into psychology but its easy to overcome a 4 foot wave, 10 foot is a bit more difficult.

As we watched through the van windows, it seemed deceptively slow, it peeled left and right perfectly.

A low pressure system had just drifted off the top of Scotland and delivered this.

We decided to paddle out through the harbour and behind the break, rather than risk breaking our necks climbing over the rocks.

In no time at all, we were in the line up.

No-one else in.

We watched a set roll through.

I sat on my board thinking this is a lot bigger and faster than it looked.

The next set, Tom caught the first wave, he swooshed, (O.K. I know its not a proper word but that's the sound he made), down the face.

I looked for my wave.

Not the second, the third in the set looked good, a bit slower... I paddled and dropped down the face, the speed of this lumbering giant surprised me.

I bottom turned and went straight up the face, through the lip and cartwheeled over the top.

Now I was buzzing.

The next couple of sets, Tom seemed to pick off with ease, I seemed to miss my wave, one or two extra strokes and I would have been there.

Again my paddling let me down, lack of surf fitness or too much beer.

I moved my position paddling about ten feet to my left, again Tom caught the first wave of the set, I paddled for the second.

On my feet, the wave seemed to double up then kick out, I was thrown forward off the board.

I tried to grab it but ended up grabbing thin air.
Again everything went into super slow-motion.
I hit the bottom of the wave, landing on my back.
My board pirouetting through the air.
I was sucked up as the huge lip broke on top of me.
I was drilled backwards until I hit the rocky bottom, (head and shoulder).
I bounced around a bit and felt I was being held down.
Thoughts at the time went-
O.K. I'm underwater I should be coming up soon...(no panic yet)
Who's holding me down, Tom was heading the other way...(still no real panic)
Seconds seemed to pass then I panicked just a bit, I kicked I struggled I shook my head, (don't panic)
I stopped struggling, I needed another breath.
As I broke the surface and gasped huge lungfulls of air, it suddenly dawned on me that 8 foot kelp (seaweed) had held me down for those few seconds.
I got drilled again, held inside for two full sets.
Eventually, I got my board back and headed for safety, "out back."

The rest of the session was really uneventful, apart from when we went for a couple of beers in the harbourside bar.
As we walked in, the music stopped all the locals turned and stared, it was like something out of American Werewolf in London. We had one pint and returned to friendlier parts.

About a year later we returned to S'land, to find similar conditions.
As we got changed we saw as a lone surfer approached, Turkey Mick, with blood oozing from a head wound, coming towards us.
"It's getting really heavy out there, had some good rides and a couple of brilliant wipe outs" he said.
We just stood and looked.
He was totally oblivious to the damage that he had done to himself.
Big globs of blood fell.
His fin had caught him behind his ear, leaving a deep nasty cut and his ear partially detached, flapping in the wind.
At the local coastguard station, he was patched up with a lot of bandage and told to go straight to hospital.

I am happy to say that I had an excellent, uneventful session.

RUNSWICK BAY WIPEOUT

On a horrendous day for surf, along the East coast, the only possible place to get a wave was at Runswick bay.

Everywhere else was just big and messy.

We piled into two vans and made our way there. Dropping down the steep bank, we saw the beach break and the outside reef both working.

It was hard at that point to tell what size the waves were.

We got changed and charged in. We surfed the beach break in the centre of the bay about 200 metres out. The waves were big and powerful but very surfable.

After 20 minutes, Tom was trying to talk people into paddling across the bay to surf the outside reef.

He convinced Rssy but the rest of us were happy where we were.

We could see it was massive over on the outside reef but the usual in check egos were let loose.

Before they set off I shouted over to Tom half in jest

"Can I have your van if you don't come back?"

Tom replied "you know where the keys are", he and Rossy then paddled off.

The reef was a good half mile paddle. We could make out two small dots of Tom and Rossy as they paddled over ever larger sets.

I caught a couple of waves and paddled back out.

I asked the lads if they could see them.

"Yeah there still paddling" shouted Shorty.

I scanned the bay. I saw the two dots make it over the top of a huge wave.

On the horizon I saw a huge rouge set rolling through.

The grey / black mass hit the area where Tom and Rossy were. Plumes of spray rose high into the air then came a boom as the wave exploded.

We all searched for signs of them between catching waves.

We convinced ourselves that they were O.K.

We carried on surfing.

Back to the carpark we were all getting changed.

Still no sign of them.

Someone said "Christ it looks big out there. Do you think they made it."

We all looked at each other then back out to sea.

At the far side of the bay Leggy spotted a longboard being thrown around in the shore break.

We assumed that they had given up the thought of the outside reef and were surfing the far side of the bay.

We all carried on as normal, we got changed and had cups of coffee then went to the local pub.

We sat at the front window looking out over the bay.

Tom and Rossy could now be seen sitting on the beach.

It seemed a bit strange them sitting instead of surfing or coming back to the vans. We got another round in and waited for them to walk back around the bay.

They were greeted by a lot of "where the fuck have youse two been?"

They both looked completely drained of energy, Toms board seemed a bit battered as well.

It turned out that they had been in the impact zone of the rogue set.

Tom had taken the brunt of it being hammered by the next wave as well. Thats when his leash had broke sending his board beachward.

Rossy had managed to get back on his. He tried to get to Tom so that they could ride / paddle out of the danger zone, back to safety on one board. The waves were that heavy and regular that there wasn't much chance.

Tom shouted "That he would see him on the beach", a good ½ mile swim away.

When they both made it to shore, they were completely knackered.

They collapsed on the beach in sheer exhaustion.

Toms board floated in on the crest of a shore break wave next to them.

Talking to Tom later, he reckoned that it was the closest he's been to dying.

I told him he was a selfish bastard. I could have had a split screen van.

What are friends for...

MEDICAL INFO

I used to think surfers were a hardy bunch, but having been part of a surfing community for many years. I now find myself questioning this.

Where to start: -

SURFERS EAR

A condition of the ear canal. The bony lining under the skin develops lumps which grow into the canal. This can cause partial or complete blockage. This can be quite painful. It's very common in colder waters the more you surf the more chance you have of getting surfers ear. Can be treated by antibiotics or worst case operation.

So the next time you're talking to a surfer and you think he's ignoring you he or she is probably deaf.

To prevent this use ear plugs, Gary uses Blue Tak.

SURF KNOTS

These are tumour like skin nodules or lumps, which appear just below the knee, on the tops of feet and toes. It's more a longboarders thing, especially those who knee paddle. The knots are seen as badges of honour by some; others just think that they are ugly lumps. Not fatal not that I know of.

SURFERS EYE

A bit like getting a flash from a welding set. Caused by prolonged exposure to sun glare and also seawater irritation. Not very common in the North East of England.

EAR, NOSE AND THROAT

At some time during your surfing life you will have various infections, its just one of the many hazards. Risks can be minimised if not surfing in sewage filled seas.

SURFERS RASH

Caused by wet suit rubbing at various places or if in warmer climbs the friction of bare chest on board / wax. If you're suffering buy a rash vest. Nipple rash can be very painful for days after. I can vouch for that.

HEPATITIS

Comes in many forms I've seen surfers suffer with A and B. It is a viral disease that has flu like symptoms and can also give you jaundice. So if you see a yellow surfer he may have HEP A or B. Go to the doctors to sort you out.

PIER RASH
Caused by hitting or running into the pier. Usually by mad surfers trying to shoot, go through, the pier legs while riding a wave. Worst case "Dangerous" Jeff's broken jaw as well as many wrecked egos and lots of damaged boards.

DROWNING
Not recommended. Caused by suffocation usually while under water. Also secondary drowning can occur after a near drowning incident. Prevented by keeping your head above water...

CUTS, BRUISES, MUSCLE PULLS AND BROKEN THINGS
Preventable by sitting at home in a padded room. In reality warm up a bit, watch what you and people around you are doing, avoid big heavy objects i.e. piers, boats etc.

ICE CREAM HEAD
This feels like your head is about to explode with a million fireworks going off at once. It is a sharp intense pain. It is caused by having your head underwater, in cold sea water, (usually wintertime is worse) for too long. i.e. too much duck diving or too many wipe-outs.
Partially preventable by wearing a hood.
For the surfers who don't like wearing hoods like myself its just another wonderful part of surfing.
Preventable by surfing only in warm water...

BOARD IMPLANTS
When you come into contact, usually because of a wipeout, with a board. Auds got a really good implant at Spanish Point. She took a wipeout and broke her nose, blood everywhere. Months later she was still picking fibre glass from the board out. Not recommended.

AGE
In your mind you're a teenager or a 23 year old, you go surfing for a few hours. Next day your as stiff as a board, muscles hurting, back and shoulders knacking. Is it worth it.
Without doubt, Yes.

MISC

There is plenty of nasty stuff in the sea. The sewage problem, the wild life i.e. weaver fish which bury themselves in the sand, their barbs are very sharp and painful. Jelly fish, if stung piss on yourself or if you're that way inclined ask a friend…

NOW

Surfing has exploded around the world. Its everywhere, everyone's doing it. Surfing is officially cool.

It still takes a lot of love for the sport, and perhaps madness, to paddle out into a Winters swell anywhere on the North East coast.

Cool no, bloody freezing yes.

Surfing equipment has improved beyond belief. Wetsuits are warmer, better fitting, 'stretchier'.

Boards are lighter, tougher, almost indestructible. The choice is mind-boggling.

Even the glossy magazines have got a lot better, notably The Surfers Path, which is a totally green magazine or Pitpilot that's a British magazine with British surfers in or Drift.

Now I pick my surfing days, if its 10ft of white mush I just won't entertain it.

I still love the winter months cold crisp mornings, snow on the ground.

Its still a real buzz.

It's just a bit of a problem when you've had a 2 hour session your knackered, hands frozen (don't really like wearing gloves, haven't worn a hood for years) and your trying to get a wet wetsuit off, the zips sticking and it starts to hail...

My paddling has never been brilliant but through dogged persistence I always get there.

The clean days, a light offshore wind holding up the waves. 4-5 foot perfection are my favourite but I will surf any size as I know that I will have a laugh if nothing else.

The dawn patrol is always special, as you know that there must be hundreds of surfers doing the same thing. Getting up early, grabbing a coffee and something to eat, trying to be quiet, gearing up, trip to the local break, suiting up, entering the water before the sun comes up. Catching waves in the early morning light, always gives you a magical feeling.

Plenty of people come in for an hour then disappear to work. What a way to start a day.

Gary, the true waterman, is nearly always, the first into the waves. He has passed a lot of his skills and knowledge onto his son Evan.

Who is a brilliant surfer in his own right.

I prefer to avoid the crowds especially in the summertime.

A dawn patrol usually means you can pick any wave you like, no hassle.

There are loads of days when I get a phone call from Tom, Rossy or Jeff saying "Surfs up" or I return the favour every now and then.

I go, it doesn't matter about the conditions, it always good to get a few waves and recharge.

Most of all I love surfing with friends and family.

Gill, after a gap of 12 years, bought a new wetsuit and is back surfing again. Its now a proper family outing when we go surfing.

Recently myself, Gill and the kids went to Devon and Cornwall.

The so-called British summer never quite materialised. 2 decent sunny days 12 of rain, magic. We made the best of it.

We had just arrived in Woolacombe, Laura surprised everyone by putting on her shortie wetsuit and asking if she could go boogie boarding. We didn't need asking twice.

We all appreciated the warmer waters. Laura picked things up really quickly and only swallowed a small amount of seawater. She was having fun and we were all loving it.

In Newquay, we surfed various breaks. James loved Fistral, even though the crowds were down for the Rip Curl boardmasters.

I had to drag him out for something to eat and drink after he'd had six hours non-stop in the surf on a longboard and body board. Obviously not at the same time..

I had to laugh as he he'd almost seized up the next day.

At an uncrowded Holywell bay, we all had some real fun in the surf.
Small to medium size mellow waves, long rides, absolutely brilliant.

Over the years Saltburn has changed a bit.
The pier and venicular lift have both undergone rebuilds and refits.
The miniature railway has been moved but still provides tourists the steam experience, deep into the Valley gardens.
There are more "posh" cafes and descent places to eat.

At the bottom of the bank, we have the white elephant building housing a descent fish and chip shop, The Seaview, Surfs up cafe and Charlie Don't Surf kite shop, just around the corner is Camfield's cafe / juice bar.

Some of the pubs have cleaned up their act.

The Queens is now Windsors. Rosies went from the Bankside to Vista Mar. All very upmarket.

Other pubs have hardly changed the Marine and Ship are still as they were, with only minor alterations. The Vic does get some good bands on though.

The Ship and Vista Mar are best for wave watching.

The surfing has changed.

I could once go down to the beach and know everyone.

Now I only recognise a few.

There are definitely more women / girls taking up the sport. Which can only be a good thing.

The credit for this has to go to the surf school, Nick, Zoee and all the instructors.

Another thing that has helped, is the addition of changing facilities and showers.

Old faces turn up now and again drawn back to Saltburn's waves. Its always good catching up.

Surfing attitude has also changed, there seems to be a lack of etiquette in the water. People drop-in time after time.

That could be annoying unless you have a longboard...long live the longboard, its the future.

The carpark has lost a lot of its atmosphere. The council spoiled the craic by getting greedy and charging for parking. Not many people risk stopping overnight.

There are still a lot of the older lads surfing and its really good to catch up and share a wave or two.

Others I regularly see in various pubs, at Boro matches or around the supermarket.

Recently, 25 of us got together and went paintballing.

We quickly realised that we would have been shite in the army.

It was a good day, spent charging around woodland, shooting people and of course getting shot.

Bruises were nursed for days after the event.

I can understand why people talk so religiously about surfing, there's something that draws you in.

To discover your true surfing soul takes time but is, without doubt, worth it.

Or maybe it's because you can chill out and relax. It's a brilliant stress reliever.

I don't know what the future holds but I do know I will always ride my longboard, hopefully surfing with family and friends.

I can't wait for Global warming to reach Saltburn waters, it will make the whole surfing experience a lot easier.

When the kids are a bit older, I definitely want to take them on a random surfing tour of Great Britain, finding the, out of the way odd secret spots as well as the more well known ones. Before some of the magazines give it all away.

So if you happen to see me in the water, paddle over say hello and we'll catch some waves together.

I know I will back in the water very soon with Gill, James, Laura and a maybe few of the old crew.

Just to bring you right up to date, myself and Dangerous Jeff were sat out back at Saltburn.

It was the start of a new swell, 3-4 foot waves, light offshore wind and believe it or not the sun was out.

There weren't many in, as it was a weekday and most people were at work.

As we waited for a set to come through, Jeff pointed and started laughing at six lads who were heading towards the water.

They were in wetsuits, dragging their Swell foam boards behind them, making a hell of a racket on the near deserted beach.

We could hear stuff like "Fucking hell, did you see that fucking wave, it was a big bastard."

Their language was colourful but their enthusiasm was infectious.

They charged in.

For ½ an hour we surfed and watched their frantic efforts.

I caught a wave in and got talking to their instructor Comcast Richie.

It turned out that they were from a school in Grangetown, (not the nicest of places but honest), a bunch of 15 year olds given time off to go surfing. That never used to happen.

As we talked some caught waves. All of them never stopped talking.

"Did you see that, I got barrelled!"

"I'm tellin ya it was clean over my head, it was a monster."

I got a sudden flashback to when we all started surfing, I recognised that same mental attitude and the same unbreakable enthusiasm.

I wondered if any of the lads would be surfing in 25 years time.

Thanks for taking time to enter my surfing life...see you in the water.

Over the years I've learnt a few things:

1. Surfing isn't about the biggest wave or the longest barrel. Its about having fun, so enjoy it.

2. Remember, there's always another wave.

3. Drunken, nude, night surfing sessions aren't really a good idea.

4. Pier's are usually made of hard stuff, avoid.

5. After a wipeout don't panic. Breathe.

6. This sounds a bit hippyish but its true "let yourself be one with nature and you will find your surfing soul."

7. Be patient and respect others in the water.

8. Be confident in your ability.

9. It's not unusual to be afraid when your surfing. Try and use the fear to your advantage.

10. Just do it. You will be surprised what you will discover about life, the universe and everything.

Acknowledgements

Thanks to all my family and friends who have helped me, knowingly or not with this book.

Thanks for the many hours, usually in a pub, going over so many old stories.

Thanks for the photos from many sources, too many to include.

It's been a nightmare and a pleasure sorting them out.

I don't know what they are all going to look like, in black and white, I had to do it this way to keep the costs down.

Thanks also to you for getting this far in the book, I hope it has either raised a smile, brought back some memories or inspired you to get into surfing.

If you didn't like it, I don't really care, I look forward to reading your book.

Take it easy,
Got to go and check the surf...

FEW OLD FACES OR ROGUES GALLERY

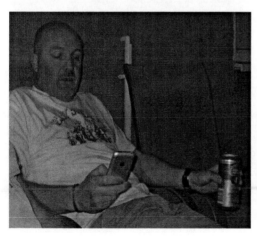

Lightning Source UK Ltd.
Milton Keynes UK
UKOW031833270613

212920UK00017B/866/P